Yours for S

A Men

By

James Halliday

For Jarvis

For [illegible] & [illegible].

In gratitude for so many years & so much friendship.

Jimmy.

22 October 2011

Scots Independent (Newspapers) Ltd

Also by James Halliday

World in Transformation – America

Scotland the Separate

Story of Scotland (co-author)

Scotland: A Concise History BC to 1990

The 1820 Rising – The Radical War

British Library Cataloguing in Publication Data
A catalogue for this book is available from the British Library

Published by
Scots Independent (Newspaper) Ltd
51 Cowane Street
Stirling
FK8 1JW
Scotland
www.scotsindependent.org

ISBN: 978-0-9512820-9-0

Printed by Peters Design & Print
Tel. (01888) 563589

Jimmy Halliday

Jimmy Halliday is unable to remember a time when he was not a Nationalist. He used to read the Scots Independent in the Greenock Public Library on the way home from school, and he joined the SNP in 1943 when he turned 16.

He graduated in history at Glasgow University, and taught in Ardeer, Coatbridge, Uddingston and Dunfermline. In 1967 he joined the History Department of Dundee College of Education, and retired in 1988 as head of that department. He has written extensively on history and the teaching of the subject; in 1990 he wrote "Scotland – A Concise History - BC to 1990"

In 1956 he was elected as the youngest ever Chairman of the Scottish National Party, aged 29, preceded by Dr Robert McIntyre, and succeeded in 1960 by Arthur Donaldson. He then became a Vice President of the Party for a number of years, chairing the Election Committee.

During Jimmy's stint as SNP Chairman the Scots Independent was formed into a limited company by the SNP; he was one of its first Directors, and is still Chairman of the paper. He lives in Broughty Ferry, Dundee.

Owen Dudley Edwards writing in "The Drouth":

We should all cherish heroes: I cherish Jimmy Halliday now in his early eighties and still the quiet implacable embodiment of a Scottish nationalism truly rooted in the values of Abraham Lincoln and Franklin Roosevelt and Martin Luther King, gorgeous mocker of Scots pseudo-Anglos and Scots Anglophobia, master analyst of Scots politics in the early eighteenth or mid-twentieth centuries, ironist and idealist, lover of life and laughter.

My simplest answer as to why and how Scottish nationalism has endured since the 1930s to the present , anti-racist and anti-militarist, would be "Jimmy Halliday". He did great things, though he makes little of them, but beyond all his accomplishments is what he was and is. If the SNP is great, it is because it has been home to a quiet, sardonic, realist philanthropist and he almost unconsciously wove his own spirit around his fellow members far beyond the realisation of most of them.

Foreword

I do not regard these reminiscences as a book. The events and developments during the years covered in the story have been examined, and narrated in scholarly fashion, by others. In particular the years of my chairmanship, and the issues and problems of these times, have been properly recorded by Dr Paula Somerville in her Strathclyde University thesis. The later years of my participation have been definitively chronicled by Gordon Wilson.

My intention was to leave a personal report which might be of some interest for later researchers. As others before me have done I have left too late the writing of a proper book. In my younger years I didn't find the time. Now I don't have the years. My memories will go, with such documentation as I have retained, into the keeping of archivists.

My thanks are due to Libby and Gregor in Dundee for their assistance, ably facilitated by Kate Young.

Alexander III

As a Nationalist and a historian, Jimmy Halliday has a profound appreciation of the significance of Alexander III, and the events unleashed by his untimely death at Kinghorn in 1286. The lack of a successor meant that the Scottish Court sought the advice of an arbiter, and found a good and fair man, they thought, in Edward of England. He then attempted to assert suzerainity over the Scots, leading to the Wars of Independence, and England only desisted when his son, also Edward was defeated at the Battle of Bannockburn in 1314. However, suzerainity over the Scots is still exercised by London to this day.

CHAPTER 1

SIGNING ON

They always ask, "Why?" "Why are you a Nationalist and why did you join the SNP?" I have never been able to offer an answer to anyone who feels that an answer is necessary. I cannot remember a time when I was not a Nationalist, even as a child. It was something automatic to me, like growing older and learning more. You just were a Scot and Scots should rule their own country. If anyone was odd, it was the person who did not see this simple truth.

The instinct was there, inborn it seems, and was not created by example or instruction. No-one ever preached nationalism to me until I was old enough to preach it to others. Neither parent ever expressed support. Almost otherwise in fact, because my mother worried all her days about what damage my opinions might be doing to my career. No adult, no teacher, no-one at all started me on my train of thought.

It might seem to others that I read my way to my convictions, but they've got it the wrong way round. I went looking for writing which encouraged the opinions which I had already decided were mine. They were the opinions, in my mind, of anyone with any notion of justice, truth and fairness.

When I was given as a birthday present – 7th I think – an abridged, illustrated edition of Scott's "Tales of a Grandfather", it was because my parents knew it would give me great pleasure. I did not learn to be a Nationalist from reading it; I read it because I already was one.

In school – Primary 3 – we were allowed to take on a Friday afternoon, a book from the class cupboard. Every Friday I took something called "Macmillan's History of Scotland" or some such vague title. The teacher, mildly irritably, suggested I might choose something else some time, but in that year I never did.

1

In that year we went from Skelmorlie School to Largs and then in the train to Ayr and there we were allowed to watch a rehearsal of the "Pageant of Ayrshire" put on for the children of the county. Different districts provided the actors for the various episodes and a highlight of my life was, and remains, travelling back in the train in a compartment full of Vikings from West Kilbride, wearing pullovers and brimless old bowler hats, all sprayed with silver paint, and the hats with horns and wings sticking out from the crowns. Few pageants must have made such an impact.

Influences were not all study-based. Until devolution, Scotland's name and existence were admitted and acknowledged by the rest of the world, only when 11 Scots played football in Scotland's colours. Anyone who thinks Scottish obsession with football is strange or out of proportion to a game's importance should reflect upon that fact.

So, my emotion was no doubt strengthened as in 1932 I wept while England beat Scotland 3-0 at Wembley. Unable to bear it, I retreated to the kitchen, re-joining the grown-ups every so often with the tearful query, "Any more goals?" 1933 at Hampden was much better. We won 2-1 and Jaikie Jackson, the Partick Thistle goalkeeper became my first sporting hero, still revered.

As for "serious politics", I remember in 1931 as the big beautiful coffee-brown Daimler of my father's employer, halted at the gate so that my parents could join the other domestic staff to go to the polling place in Inverkip, where it was taken for granted they would vote for H.J. Scrimgeour-Wedderburn, the Conservative candidate. They probably did, though John Campbell the chauffeur had been in the United States, bringing back with him a copy of Bellamy's "Looking Backward. When Socialism comes." The copy was passed around chauffeurs and gardeners, postmen and railwaymen, in our community, and I recall my father looking thoughtfully into the middle distance after some readings.

2

In 1935, at the General Election, I heard mention of a candidate for West Renfrewshire, called R.E. Muirhead, who was described as a "Scottish Nationalist", probably the earliest use of the term I had heard. Nobody knew or bothered much about Mr Muirhead's message, whatever it was. All I can recall being said of him then, and for years thereafter, was that he had refused to pay his tithes. What these were, and what his obligations had been, neither then nor now do I know, but Mr Muirhead was forever politically disadvantaged by the gaffe, whatever it was.

The election had been fought to some extent on the record of the "National" Government – (ie Tory with some renegades from the Labour and Liberal parties) in governing throughout the tensions of the time, mass unemployment, means testing and hunger marches. The overwhelming view, incredibly enough, was that the Tories had done splendidly. At a Wemyss Bay Social Club whist drive on an evening shortly before the election, I heard one young lady's voice raised in explanation of why a Labour win was quite unthinkable. "They have," she declared, "no brains".

The other election issue of the time was British diplomacy, in particular the handling of the crisis caused by the Italian invasion and occupation of Abyssinia. Italians were assumed to be in the wrong, and when the fugitive Emperor of Abyssinia, Haile Selassie, came to spend part of his exile at Castle Wemyss, he was cheered by a small but sympathetic crowd, mostly mothers and children, to whom the little Emperor, sad no doubt but smiling, raised his top hat as his car passed through the Castle gate. His visit seemed to bring the world closer, and of course from then on everyone was caught up in the approach to war.

Italian military power revealed itself again in Spain when the civil war broke out there in 1936. We incorporated this latest conflict into our games, which until then had been nearly unbroken re-runs of the Great War, as we re-enacted the scenes which our fathers never talked about.

On social occasions, Spain came in for attention too. It was the tradition in the circle of my parents' friends that each family would host a party for all the others, starting early in the New Year and extending week by week usually until March. On one such occasion two of the men worked out, and presented, a short sketch in which one played the part of Prime Minister Chamberlain and the other, a citizen seeking information. British ships had been halted by warships of the Spanish navy, fighting on the rebel side, and British families were alarmed by the possibility of incidents which might lead to bloodshed.

The "concerned citizen" in the sketch was Willie Moffat, the gardener in the property next door to that where my father was gardener. Willie's arrival had pleased my father greatly, because they had met previously in 1917 during the campaign defending Salonika in the Struma Valley. Willie took a poor view of British statecraft, and in the script which he provided he gave his Chamberlain character the comforting lines, "Never mind if the Spanish cruisers sink a few of our boats. The ships are obsolete, and the men are Communists." So that's all right then.

The Conservative defeat in 1945 was to a great extent dictated by these events which I watched unfold in the 30s.

In 1938 on my way to the Greenock bus and school, I used to meet an unemployed man who came down daily from Greenock to join his friends spending their days in and near huts which they had built from driftwood along the shore towards Gourock. We had a brief daily discussion on politics as the Munich crisis developed. My discussant deplored Britain's abandoning of the country which he called "Checko-Slekovakey." An alternative point of view was displayed by our Scoutmaster, who sang, as he drove a carload of us Sea Scouts to Coulport, the praises of Mr Chamberlain, the "Umbrella Man" as the Flanagan & Allen song put it, who had given peace and safety to us all.

1938 saw Glasgow hosting the Empire Exhibition in Bellahouston Park. There was the Tower, the Clachan, the Victoria Falls replica and pavilions displaying the products and aspects of society of all the various dominions and colonies of the Empire. After some searching among the stalls I found what I had sought, a modest little stall offering leaflets and pamphlets, pens and pencils, postcards and souvenirs and lapel badges where I bought my first Scottish National Party badge, though I was not yet a member. At the age of 11 I felt that I was not quite eligible, but five years later, when I presumed I would be old enough to be accepted, I joined. Being old enough was all the motive or reason I needed. The badge is big and clumsy by modern artistic standards, and has the old unsubtle design of the rampant lion superimposed upon the Saltire. On the back it says "Empire Exhibition: Glasgow 1938." In my own eyes that is when I joined. I still have the old badge and value it highly.

The outbreak of the long-threatened war in 1939 was a political disaster for the party. A feeling of unity spread throughout Britain intensifying as time passed and set backs increased public notion of danger. People saw themselves as members of a garrison, a ship's company, a battalion, a squadron. Though not personally in action, civilians regarded themselves as serving somehow behind the lines. As well as this emotional sense of unity, and to a conscious degree reflecting it, British political parties entered into an electoral truce, which encouraged the feeling that anyone breaking that truce was really somehow disloyal.

The SNP was not bound by the agreement, having no representation in Parliament anyway, so its leaders regarded themselves as being still at liberty to contest elections. This they did in 1940, when William Power was their candidate in a by-election in Argyll, where he secured a very creditable vote. The Party's continuing wish to fight the political battle was not in most cases prompted by opposition to participate in the war. Some members did take this view. Those who had been pacifist in their opinions pre-war continued, many of them, to hold these opinions.

From a specifically Scottish point of view there was a considerable degree of opposition to conscription. Some argued that the terms of the Union did not entitle Parliament in London to conscript Scots. Opposition became stronger and more bitter when the conscription of women, and compulsory direction of labour, compelled Scottish women to submit to taking jobs in English and England based factories.

I can recall no display of support for any idea that Scottish independence could ever be derived from a British defeat. Irish nationalism had once benefitted from the notion that "England's difficulty is Ireland's opportunity". But Irish nationalism had a foundation in hatred of England which Scots had never seriously felt, or sought to use.

So, Nationalist opinion was, it seemed, mainly supportive of Britain and the British war effort, and the SNP leaders took this view. There had been, from around 1937 a body called the Scots Neutrality League, which continued to function with the support and, to a degree, the leadership, of Nationalist personalities, notably Arthur Donaldson. Arthur's views had obviously attracted the attention of British security forces, and earned him a period of detention in prison, until wiser politicians like Tom Johnstone and James Maxton, who knew him, brought about his release.

Another detainee, briefly, a future Secretary of the SNP, and a future holder of a British military commission, was Muriel Gibson. Party legend tells of Muriel's mother shouting warnings to the persons removing her daughter, under arrest, "Be sure you bring that girl back exactly as she was when you took her." Both ladies in later years recalled the moment with great satisfaction.

In 1942 internal dissension within the Party came to a head when William Power was opposed in the Annual Conference elections, by Douglas Young, who had attracted the admiration and excitement of many members, by his refusal to submit to conscription and had been imprisoned as a result. When Power was defeated, and Young became chairman, John MacCormick, who had supported Power, resigned as National Secretary on the spot and, joined by those who saw matters as he did, began a meeting in nearby premises which established the Scottish Convention.

The story of the Convention, and of its later identity as the Scottish Covenant Association, is now long familiar. Familiarity does not always imply accuracy, however, and the story that the Convention was loyal to Britain while the SNP was neutralist is far from a full explanation of the split of 1942.

There had been from the Party's earliest days, a probability that lack of success in continued challenges and confrontations of the British parties, would dishearten many, and incline them to seek out other means to their political ends. The Home Rule Association had always sought to progress by consensus, conversion and co-operation. The Scottish Party, had shown a distaste for the more militant stance of the National Party, and these sentiments still influenced not a few members of the SNP, who came from these traditions.

In particular, there was the questioning and active mind of John MacCormick, who could see that prospects of independence being won by General Election successes was so far beyond imagining as to be impossible. He therefore sought to re-think strategy, and his answer was to place the campaign for independence above party loyalties and call upon all sympathisers to give the objective their support without shedding their own personal partisan opinions. As a tactic it made much sense. It placed minimal demands upon supporters and removed the need to make hurtful choices in politics.

In the next few years Convention had all the known leaders, any money that was available, the attention of the press and the goodwill of the respectable. It was the organisation, so people were led to believe, of moderate, temperate, realistic Nationalism, and it was loyal in support of the war effort. The SNP on the other hand was presented to the public as extremist, obsessive and perhaps disloyal. In winning friends and influencing people, there was really no contest.

For my part, even though approaching the age for military service, I never for an instant supported the notion of neutrality. The war was, as they now say, a Good War, against

7

monstrous threats to human freedom. It was my war, it was Scots' war as much as anyone else's.

But it wasn't all a matter of emotion. It was about realism and a readiness to be taught by both History and Geography. Neutrality was no defence against invasion, as Denmark, Belgium and Holland had already learned, not having had the sense to realise their vulnerability in advance. Scotland, sharing the land mass of Great Britain with England, could not escape any Power's temptations to take strategic advantage of ports, harbours, products and amenities which an attacker might feel useful.

If any proof were needed, we saw that it wasn't just Germany which broke its neighbours' bounds if the need arose. Neutrality didn't enable Iceland to keep out British, and, in due course, American forces. They may have come as allies, and certainly as a lesser evil, but resident allies came all too quickly to look very like an army of occupation.

So I was willing to choose to join the fight, but I knew in addition, that none of us was given any real choice. With or without our consent, our involvement was inescapable. So I sided in my mind with John MacCormick in so far as he sought to guide Nationalists away from neutrality or pacifism. That did not mean that I agreed then or at any later date with the sanction-less strategy which he had given Convention.

Most of these events had been outwith my awareness. I knew of William Power since 1940 but the issues behind the 1942 break-up were beyond me.

I had been finding Nationalist information however. On my way home from school I'd pick up the bus to Inverkip from the bus stop at Westburn Square, where a branch of Greenock Public Library had in its Reading Room, the modest 4-page journal, "Scots Independent." From the SI I learned about the SNP's issues, persons and events.

I found an understandable book on the economic possibilities in an independent Scotland, "The Scotland of our Sons", and a surprisingly detailed plan of possible structure of government in "The Thistle and The Rose", by Sir Alexander McEwen. I read all these sources of information. In the SI I found mention of pamphlets by names which I came to recognise – Arthur Donaldson, Archie Lamont and Oliver Brown. This was all most encouraging.

But, in all this time and all through these, my schooldays, not one contemporary acquaintance shared my point of view, or ever said a supportive word. Some Nationalists had existed in Greenock to be sure. There was John L. Kinloch, once an office bearer in the SNP but now pretty much a Labour loyalist, teaching in Greenock Academy and enrolling some of his pupils in a youth organisation "Clan Scotland" which despite its name was not visibly active in politics.

Two teachers influenced me profoundly. One of them, Dewar Robb, taught English with a degree of enthusiasm and professional skill which I don't think could have been surpassed anywhere. I have certainly never heard anyone speak of their English teacher with such gratitude and admiration as I have felt for Robb. I later came to realise that he had some nationalist sympathies. He was related to Dewar Gibb of the SNP, and now Convention, and to J.M. Reid, the well known, well regarded Editor of the "Bulletin", the famous stablemate of the "Glasgow Herald", but allowed to deviate from the suburban, mammon-revering, plutocratic journal which the "Herald" then was.

The other, who was teacher of History, and exemplar to me, was Archibald Duncan. Anyone with the surname "Duncan" to boys in the 30s immediately was awarded the nickname "Dally", because Scotland's outside left, greatest probably apart from Alan Morton, was Dally Duncan of Derby County.

Dally was all that a teacher could be. A great enthusiast for his subject, humorous to a degree, and unfailingly good humoured, he was highly popular and highly influential. He was a man who was politically well informed and interested. He alone made any

9

comment to me about the SNP. He was not hostile, but not positively sympathetic either. He did however remark that the SNP suffered from the fact that only one of its leading figures revealed any political skill – John MacCormick.

So school had not given me any great encouragement in any party loyalty. Some mildly political events occurred. In my sixth year, having moved on from the Highers in 5th year, I was free to do a fair number of hours in private study. The idea then seemed to grow, and I spread it around, that we might have a Debating Society in the school. There had been one, but it had fallen into disuse, so with the help of James McCrorie of the English department, we re-started it. I tried to find opportunities to make converts, but there were no takers.

So I read. Dewar Robb was a marvellous man to point the young along interesting paths. As well as class work, where we read all the usual exam relevant authors, I was encouraged in appreciating two contrasting schools of poetry, the Romantics and the Augustans. For years I believed that Shelley was the only real poet, but Pope and Dryden could entertain by the sheer skills of language. Burns was of course a favourite, and Shaw's "St Joan" made a summer term rewarding. I read my way through most of the novels, and poems, of Walter Scott, historical novelist par excellence. Finest was, surely, "The Heart of Midlothian", but I was most moved by the novels set in the 17th Century, - "Redgauntlet", for "Wandering Willie's Tale", but especially "Old Mortality". I was already committed in my support of those who resisted the Crown. Drumclog, Bothwell Bridge, and, finally, Dunkeld were most revered landmarks. I was on the opposite side from Cavalier and Royalist Scott, but his use of these historical events fascinated.

Dally pointed to History works in the Library, but he knew a bit about historical novels too. "The Herries Chronicle" he recommended, and I found Upton Sinclair and Sinclair Lewis among American authors to be followed. In History proper, Dally gave me an opportunity which I never heard of being on offer in any other school. In the last term at school he had his Higher class and me (they being a year younger) study the history of the United States. So it was that, by the time I went to University, I knew the essential

10

formative periods and landmarks in American history. This I added to the European history from about 1780 till as near to the present as we could reach.

The lifelong conviction about politics, which I cling to, was based upon the developments in Europe in the mid 1800s. In 1848 the text books tell us, European Monarchs and empires were challenged by the forces of liberalism and nationalism. Italians, Magyars, Slavs, all of them subjects of empires which were alien as well as dictatorial, rose in revolt to demand political liberty and national independence. Though 1848 was only a rehearsal, it established the principle which to me has been the obviously just guide to our aspirations.

I have long realised that generations who never knew wartime can never understand those of us who lived through these years. Looking at dates in History books, the years from the dawn of recorded time to the year of my birth were accepted without meaning very much. From 1927 till 1939 I enjoyed an ordinary enough childhood. Looking back, the years from 2010 till 1945 have gone in a flash, but the years from 1939 till 1945 have seemed endless. I suppose that's what people mean by "formative years". As far as my own political likes and dislikes are concerned they all have their roots and their debating sources in those years. In world controversies and internal Party disagreements, I find judgement and guidance in the cast of mind which I formed then, and I confess to much bewilderment and impotence when colleagues fail to see things which I find obvious.

I don't accept as so many now do, that good and evil are just a matter of opinion or mere prejudice. I don't accept that you must always be ready to ridicule and denounce your friends while seeking every chance to excuse your enemies. I don't believe that you are showing great breadth of mind if you reverse Holy Writ, and claw furiously at the speck in your own eye, while ignoring the plank in the eye of a bully. I can't accept that you must act as though Communist Gulags should be brushed into oblivion because rich Americans are often promiscuous. A sense of proportion and an appreciation of comparative villainies should be borne in mind.

And you don't get peace by milling around shouting "Peace", and you don't get "Justice" with banners.

Sad though it might be, a degree of selfishness must be taken for granted. For instance, I believe that instinct, perfectly defensible, will prompt any nation to save the lives of its own children in preference to those of an enemy when the choice has to be made. Any leader who does that will have the agreement of his own people. Any leader who in a fine flurry of self-denial chooses otherwise will be overthrown, and rightly so. Whole organisations, given to virulent moralising, may, and do, disagree, but I remember these war years and believe my conclusions are logical and defensible.

We are terrified by the constant threat of atomic warfare. Why are we so terrified? Because we know what it would be like. How do we know? Because it has already happened. A dreadful, hard lesson for all powers and peoples, but better then than since and better there than elsewhere.

Some lessons were taught by wartime experiences closer to home. Greenock as a major naval port saw ships at anchor, troopships bringing soldiers from Canada and South Africa, Australia and New Zealand, and, eventually, Americans, to be found in the town's streets. Dutch and Polish servicemen passed through, and French naval pickets with bayonets fixed were summoned on occasion to clear their misbehaving colleagues from scenes of scuffles.

In June 1940, a shameful evening to look back upon, came when riotous mobs took ignorant revenge for Italy's declaration of war in an orgy of destruction of Italian cafes and chip shops. To see small children with hammers, sitting trying to bash their way into the slot machines' money boxes made me afraid of what lawlessness could be called upon by any body unscrupulous enough to issue the call.

Most lingering of all of course, is the memory of the air raids on Greenock in May 1941. Even today I find myself wondering why there is no longer debris piled up in the gutters, while burning beams lay across Ann Street, where women in shawls stood loudly denouncing Churchill and demanding peace. War's lessons are not always flattering.

In 1943 I was of an age to register for war service. At least one Party colleague has asked if I never sought or expected to escape the call. It was probably just a matter of resigned acceptance rather than enthusiasm, but it was, to those at the time, as mere normality. On registering I requested to be sent to the Navy, not from any feeling of heroism, but a very lively wish not to be sent to Burma, which was the destination of most army recruits of the time. As it happened, I had no need to scheme.

I had in my last months at school sat the Glasgow University Bursary exam, and those who had performed acceptably were given a year's deferment of service, allowing them to have one year at University before being taken into the services. This meant that I was able to begin studies in Glasgow in October 1944.

Studies were on the whole enjoyable, but most satisfaction for me was to meet up at least, for the first time, with other Nationalists, in the University's Scottish Nationalist Association. Its Honorary Officials included Compton MacKenzie, Krishna Menon of the Indian National Congress, Saunders Lewis of Plaid Cymru, Hugh McAteer, Irish Republican, D.F. Malan, South African Afrikaner leader and, as if there wasn't enough potential for rows in that line-up , C.M. Grieve, Hugh MacDiarmid.

Clearly the Association was on what the outside world would have described as the extremist wing of Nationalism.

The student committee members however, were a perfectly reasonable and cheerful lot. The President, Brendan Donnachie, was a very witty and articulate fellow, much admired in the Union as an entertaining and thoughtful speaker. The Association's critics liked to describe Brendan as "Dictator, Scot. Nat. Club". He was the most colourful perhaps, but the others had their merits.

13

For instance, one young man on the committee I looked upon with awe. In 1944 the Party, despite the Convention's impact upon public expectations, had decided to contest a by-election in Kirkcaldy. As in Argyll, a surprisingly good vote was secured by the Party's nominee, its Chairman, Douglas Young. And one of our committee members was pointed out to me as having been Douglas Young's election agent! This was surely politics in full bloom. I later learned that he would have been more precisely described as "Assistant Election Agent", the full title going to the more experienced man who had actually run the campaign, Arthur Donaldson.

We were not strong numerically, and for that very reason I found myself speaking in debates for the club. My first crit, as printed in the Clerk of the House's report advised "Speak up son. You're promising." I felt slightly upset at the implication of youth, but otherwise contented.

In the Union, lunch time meetings were addressed by political notables of various sorts. Gavin Henderson, a History lecturer, returned on leave to tell the story of the Cairo Forces Parliament, where left-wing opinions among those attending led to the abrupt closure of the whole thing. Arnold Lunn, explorer, mountaineer and pugnacious Catholic publicist, was invited by the Distributist Club to have his say, which he did with much skill. His presence in sectarian Glasgow caused some growlings even in a University.

Of greatest interest to me was the appearance of Hector McNeil, MP for Greenock. He had been successful in a by-election in which some of my school friends had worked for him. He had gathered together a meeting of senior pupils and their teachers, at which I met John L. Kinloch, to whom I revealed my Nationalist opinions. I was not as well received as I expected, as Kinloch's Nationalist sympathies had diminished markedly since his days as SNP Secretary. McNeil then attended the High School prize-giving, when I had the pleasure of being awarded the English Prize which he had financed. When he turned up in the Union several of us from Greenock and thereabouts went along to lend our support. His topic was the civil war in Greece, where the German withdrawal had left rival militias to fight it out for mastery. I felt that the British government,

14

following the traditional Foreign Office path of diplomacy, always tried desperately to find any excuse to support a monarchy, no matter how unsavoury. Mr McNeil took much the same point of view. Oddly enough when he returned as a British Minister in 1948 he took the opposite point of view, which thus seemed to prove the justice of my assessment of any official British party line.

In February the Union debate was focussed mainly upon the Yalta Agreement, whereby the British, with little choice in the matter, had abandoned Poland and Eastern Europe in general to the mercies of the Soviet Union. The Distribs were bursting with anger, and in their heated state ranged in speeches, far beyond Yalta and into the plight of Catholic Europe in general. Willie Glen, a Glasgow lawyer, who was alleged to have served somehow in Franco's armies in Spain, was a marvellous orator, who became quite lyrical in his recalling the defence of the Alcazar. A colleague of his, a Mr Ommer, who was, I think, a medical student, referred with great fervour to "the blood-stained paw of the Soviet bear", and was expelled from the debate for this insult to an ally! Strange to recall perhaps, but those were the days when Russian military missions were met in London railway stations by crowds who cheered, sang the "Internationale", and carried the Red Army Generals shoulder high. Even popular songs showed how opinion tended. "Russian Lullaby", and "My Lovely Russian Rose" were broadcast repeatedly for quite some time.

It was all very exciting and I was thoroughly enjoying myself.

That February was my swan-song in the University. For over a year I had been feeling increasingly unfit, always tired and increasingly in pain. At Christmas of 1944 I found myself unable to walk from the serving counter into the smoking room in the Union. My old school classmate, Harry McGilp, now a second year medical student, came with me in the train to Inverkip and I was recovered enough to get home from the station.

When the new term began in January I was able to return to classes and to the Union. At the time I travelled from home daily, and on, I think, the 18th of February, I got off the

15

tram and climbed the steps into the Union, where I was met by a very serious GUSNA colleague, Hamish McIntosh, he of the Kirkcaldy by-election, who pointed to his black tie. He quickly explained its significance. When my complaints of pain were considered by our doctor back home, he sent me to the Western Infirmary for investigation and X-rays. Another out-patient was Brendan Donnachie, who had some undiagnosed problem. So, Brendan and I had swapped notes and thoughts in the Western's waiting rooms as our ailments were investigated. In due course, Brendan had been sent for surgery, and as Hamish's black tie now indicated, he had died in the theatre.

With this news I returned home and was met, most unusually, at the bus stop by my mother. She had worried about me for a couple of years, and she had been given further worry when my father was taken into the Greenock Eye Infirmary where he was to remain for some weeks. While he was a patient there, his father, my grandfather, died, and I had to take what should have been my father's role in the funeral. It was thoughtless, but like most boys, little more than children, I was full of talk about Brendan, but was swiftly silenced as my mother told me that the doctor had been, and had ordered that I must immediately take to bed and stay there until admission to hospital could be arranged.

For three glorious spring weeks I lay and looked out over the Clyde as far down as the Cumbrae, where for all the war years we had watched convoys come and go. Now I just marvelled at the beauty of the Firth and its hills, and waited. In early March an ambulance took me to Fairlie pier to be carried on the "Glen Sannox" to Millport, where St Andrew's Home dealt with patients who were suffering, as it was now known, like me, from tuberculosis of the spine.

I didn't stand up again until June 1947. I was in an ambulance again in May 1946 when I had to be rushed to Greenock Royal Infirmary for a life-saving operation for peritonitis. The surgeon in Greenock, Alexander Lyall, saved me, and I returned to Millport, there to remain until discharged in July 1947.

So it came about that I was encased in a plaster shell, flat on my back, when Robert McIntyre won the by-election in Motherwell in April 1945. I rejoiced of course, and when the S.I. appeared with its victory headline, I put it up above my bed to display our triumph. No one else of course was pleased. The sister in charge had all the hallmarks of an authoritarian Tory who disliked me anyway as a student, likely to have far too much to say for himself. Greater was the displeasure of an English marine across the ward who wanted to fight, while, both immobile, we hurled defiant challenges across the space between us.

After Robert's victory we had little time to wait before the General Election, first since 1935. A Parliament elected to guide a British government in its dealings with the war in Abyssinia, had staggered along, landed with the responsibility of dealing with a war all over the world. Clearly it was high time that public opinion was given its chance.

Again the S.I. provided photos and information about the Party's candidates. Again West Renfrewshire had nominated a candidate, not Muirhead this time, but Robert Blair Wilkie, whose name I had seen in various items in the S.I., but who was otherwise unknown. However, I had time on my hands, and there seemed to be a job which I might possibly do. So, I wrote to HQ in Elmbank Street, offering, if the Party could send me the necessary labels, to write on them the names of all the voters in the constituency. I never heard a word in response.

The election was, as the record shows, a very disappointing experience, which was used by those who were by now anxious to avoid fighting elections.

Aside from the Party's set back, the election of a Labour government seemed to deserve welcome, and I showed elation once again to the annoyance of Ted across the ward. After all, Home Rule was an objective to which the Labour Party was committed. No one expected them to grant us independence, but it was assumed that some measure of Home Rule would be on offer.

No one could really have predicted how quickly that commitment would be rejected. No one could have foreseen the effrontery of the argument that now we had a Labour government Scotland didn't need Home Rule. From that day to this, this combination of every sort of offence against reasoned argument has been quite sufficient to provide Labour politicians with their sole sources of inspiration and dialectic.

Between Labour's victory and my discharge in 1947 "things were very tight outside" as we were always told if we expressed any grievance about our diet or conditions in general. Once I was home again I gradually caught up with the reports of what sufferings these first post war years had brought. Rationing was more severe than it had been during the war, and the bitter prolonged winter of 1946-7, when roads, rail and even sea-borne traffic were halted, had tested everyone's endurance to the full. That winter's weather I remember particularly, because my bed was next to an open doorway and I had snow from my pillow to my feet down the right-hand side which was open to the drifting snow.

Politically these hardships created much discontent and the excited enthusiasm for Labour was eroded by discontent fomented fiercely by the British press. Not being considered fit to return to University immediately, I spent a year with no great contact with public affairs, but I knew that I would be back to the University and its political life in 1948.

CHAPTER 2

UNIVERSITY POLITICS

On returning to the University in October 1948 I was quickly aware that being a student aged 21 was very different from being a student aged 17. The experiences of the years since my first arrival had made me much fitter to participate in "the corporate life", as the phrase put it. Lodging in Glasgow instead of travelling daily made a fuller range of activities available. In particular I was able, at long delayed last, to return to the Nationalist Association and to the Union.

On the Bute Hall stairs – right at the foot because GUSNA office-bearers had been too slow to grab a prominent place on the higher steps – I was invited, rather diffidently, to become a member. With some concealed glee I produced my membership card from 1944, and proffered also my Party card. Much taken aback, but rallying to express his pleasure, was David D.T. Reid, the club's President. Chortling his appreciation was the Secretary, James J. Scott who became my closest colleague and friend then, and for the rest of his life.

From David and Jarvis – ("James" caused too many irritations as being the name shared with his father) – I heard something of the club's history in those three years. It became clear that things had not gone well, and that the officials had allowed matters to drift. The one event which was remembered with modest satisfaction, was the Rectorial election of 1947. The Tories had succeeded in electing Walter Elliot. One of the unsuccessful candidates was Sir Thomas Beecham, whose campaign had proved vastly entertaining, and the other, making up a line-up of quite remarkable fame and colour, was James Bridie. GUSNA had nominated and supported Bridie, but the campaign had not left any obvious benefits. The Club had in fact got itself faced with bills for the Union's facilities, which it could not meet. As a result, all GUSNA meetings now had to take place in the QM Union.

The new leaders made it clear that they saw themselves as rejecting the former regime, but some individuals had retained their membership. One such, now a Law trainee, and no longer a constant presence in either Union, was a young woman called Winnie Woodburn. She was spoken of as being unblemished by the defects of the past and was identified to me as a person worthy of our approval. Winnie and I passed to and fro, day by day, exchanging mere courtesies, but I appreciated that she was invariably civil and pleasant.

She didn't ever appear at GUSNA meetings. Lawyers beginning their careers found few leisure hours. Still, GUSNA had a leading lady, Elspeth M. Gallie, a final year History student, very capable and confident. Unfortunately her first political loyalty was to the Liberal Party, and for her GUSNA was an optional extra.

I found that this was a very normal aspect of GUSNA membership. Only two of us were Party members, and we were both in our first year. Before Alasdair MacDonald and myself, there seemed to have been no Party members since Hamish McIntosh in 1943-44. Not only were club members not Party members, they prided themselves on the fact. Some of them, though in favour of Home Rule, had prior loyalties to British parties. David Reid was Labour, Elspeth was Liberal, as was Jarvis and another young stirring member, Gerry Fisher. Vi Thomson our Q.M. Convener was avowedly Tory in her sentiments. Even those with Nationalist sympathies reacted with distaste at any thoughts of joining the SNP. One young man who had become associated with Oliver Brown and his Scottish Socialist Party, was Robert J. Shirley. Like his mentor, Bob viewed party membership and discipline as being too restrictive of free spirits. This attitude for many a long day was commonly found in the young, who found in themselves such originality as to make Party membership seem a contemptible abandoning of personal freedom of thought. One colleague who carried freedom of thought into public expression, at some hazard to himself, was Ian Hamilton. He and Bob were of a mind in their policies and in their choice of academic course. They pursued a study of Politics and Economics, to the mystification of those of us who wondered how they would ever get jobs with such off-target subjects.

As was the usual custom, the club's main function was to prepare for, and participate in, the regular Union debates. Six such debates were held throughout the year, allowing each of the six clubs to perform as the government in turn. The Liberals had ruled the roost in the debates, as in the Union and student society generally. Their "front bench" were talented, confident, fluent and in many cases were studying subjects of obvious political relevance, economics in all forms being a particular favourite.

The Conservative Club was altogether less flamboyant and had fewer debaters with the variety of skills which the Liberals could display. Labour, as befitted the supporters in the Union of the governing party in the country, were a bit stodgy, apart from two gifted speakers. They were on the whole well versed in their politics but not blessed with apparent originality or initiative.

There was another leftist club, identified as "Socialist", retaining something of the 1944 Popular Front approach. There were avowed communists, orthodox socialists in these pre-Maoist days; one Titoist (allegedly) and various persons whose leftist views discouraged party discipline.

The Distributist Club continued to flourish, finding plenty of opportunities to publicise especially the Catholic response to world events. The detention of first, Cardinal Stepinac of Croatia, and then Cardinal Mindsczenty of Hungary, called forth much fire and eloquence from the Distributists who seemed to have lost much of their commitment to the economic enthusiasms of Chesterton and Belloc.

Then there was GUSNA. As the debating session of 1948 began, much political excitement was provided by the events arising from the founding and recognition of the state of Israel. David Reid had served in the British forces in Palestine and Iraq. Like so many British soldiers with experience in that area, he had become much attached to the Arab cause, and had formed a very critical attitude towards some of the pugnacity displayed by the Israelis in those dangerous times. For my part, carrying as always my

21

angry hostility towards imperial motivation, I took the same side as David, though for rather different reasons. As I saw it, the world's politicians had handed over to the Zionist campaigners, territory which was not theirs to give. To provide a national home in which Jews could govern and be safe was an objective ideology to be welcomed and supported, but it would have seemed much more just if the land on offer was in the legal possession of governments making the offer. That seemed logical to me then.

As the Union turned in its first debate to consider the problems involving Israel and its neighbours, I was chosen to join David in presenting a case which could be said to have Nationalist relevance. So my apprentice debating attack on British conduct in Greece in 1944 was now followed by a further attack on British conduct in the Near East. Without this issue I might not have been on our front bench team this early, but having been placed there, I stayed for the next four years.

We went into debates with a team of six. Speaking at the peak hours of the opening session in the pre-lunch period, then throughout the evening, concluding at any time dictated by interest – usually high, and sustained, with full galleries and full club benches, until the following day had begun.

David, Jarvis and I bore the brunt of the speaking. Others in turn contributed as their interests dictated. Elspeth and Vi spoke, and Bob Shirley, Gerry Fisher and Iain Wood chipped in. Coming in as experienced reinforcements, especially on some vital occasion, we could count on former club stalwart, and now Glasgow solicitor, Willie Macrae. With this line-up, GUSNA, the unsung underdogs of 1947 became debating champions and David accepted the trophy on our behalf.

In 1949 we had to share the trophy with the Labour club and Jarvis went forward in comradely association with Dick Mabon. Our office-bearer elections were very orderly. In 1948 David was President, Jarvis Secretary. In 1949 David had been elected the Union's Debates Convener, Jarvis took over as club President and I became Secretary. Jarvis had begun production of a club-sponsored booklet which he named "The Free

Scot" and he and I spent the summer of 1949 seeing to its printing in time for distribution when the new session started. This gave me my first encounter with some Nationalist believers, two brothers who did the printing and R E Muirhead whose Scots Secretariat in Elmbank Crescent provided useful texts.

In 1950 I became President and was selected as Debater of the Year. Unfortunately we were only second in the trophy race, but our continued highly-respected performance brought about my election as Convenor of Debates in the Union, following Dick Mabon in that office.

1950 however was made important to the club by activity in a wider context – the campaign to elect a new Lord Rector, Walter Elliot's term of office having expired.

As I remember, it was the Liberal club chairman, Douglas B Taylor who suggested to Jarvis that our clubs might think of jointly nominating a man who had played a leading role in founding the Scottish National Party; had come close to achieving the election as Rector of R B Cunningham Grahame; had followed along that blazed trail to prepare for the election of Compton Mackenzie; and had served as secretary and really, the mainspring, of the Scottish National Party from its earliest days until 1942, when he left to form the Scottish Convention and drew up the Scottish Covenant. This one man, John M MacCormick, had been a Liberal Party candidate, and his credentials seemed properly to appeal to both our clubs.

On many issues I would have agreed with MacCormick, particularly on his attitude towards participation in the War. But I was a Party man, and did not support his Convention-type strategy. I had always been convinced that the Unionist position had to be confronted and defied. Any less overt argument would never succeed in bringing our people to the point of decision. We had to contest elections, not because we had serious expectations of victory, but because we had no alternative if we were to persevere in our struggle towards independence.

23

However, I was fully aware that the Scottish people did not differentiate between Party and Convention. Success for either would seem in their eyes to be a success for the general campaign towards Home Rule. So it made sense to me to join in Douglas Taylor's plan.

We had had MacCormick as a guest speaker at one of the very testing Union lunch time meetings. He had spoken very well and in response to the very customary shout from the oafish corner of the hall to "give us a song", he actually obliged with a song, unfamiliar to me, but better known in former years as "To be a Clerk in an Office."

Douglas and Jarvis, as retiring club Presidents, and Ron Fraser and myself as their successors, constituted ourselves as a campaign committee, and proceeded to meet with our candidate, to secure his formal acceptance. It was not in those days, the done thing for Rectorial candidates to be actively involved or even visible in the campaign, so we dealt from then on with Bertie Gray. Bertie headed a famous monumental sculptor firm in Sauchiehall Street. He had been associated with MacCormick since the earliest days of the rising Home Rule Movement. It was Bertie who, as SNP candidate, polled so strongly in the Dumbarton constituency in the 1931 General Election, that the Labour incumbent, the famous Tom Johnston, lost the seat. Before this defeat, Tom Johnston had the seniority, popularity and general political power to have become leader of the sad little 50 strong group which was now the Parliamentary Labour party. In the imposed absence of Johnston, Labour's leadership fell to George Lansbury and then to Clement Attlee. So Bertie could be held responsible for Attlee the Prime Minister and Johnston the wartime Secretary of State for Scotland. Bertie had followed MacCormick along every political path. He left the SNP and joined the Convention and, in that all-party body, he was free to enter Glasgow's municipal politics as a Progressive councillor and in due course, a Baillie.

We now for some weeks in the autumn of 1950 planned our campaign, making frequent visits to Bertie's office. We met some of his staff, and were favoured with a chance to inspect several copies of the Stone of Destiny, which Bertie and his colleagues had made

24

just in case a use might some day be found for them. It emerged that Bertie and others unknown, had cherished an ambition to have the Stone returned to Scotland by political agreement, failing which someone some day might organise an expedition for its rescue.

We made alliances beyond our political clubs. The Distributists came on board. Frank Hamill, then chairman, joined our committee, and Gavin Henry, their most experienced student member, exercised unsuspected talents to produce one of the songs which we used in the campaign. From the outside world we brought to campaign publicity meetings in the Union, supporters to speak on our candidate's behalf. John Bannerman came along to give the Liberal seal of approval. No SNP official was invited, as the Party's open support was unlikely. Instead personalities with known or suspected Home Rule sympathies came to plead "King John's" cause. Thus we enjoyed the very effective support of Dr Tom Honeyman, the famous chief of the Art Galleries, and Duncan Macrae, the best-known Scots actor of his generation. Honeyman proved to be a brilliant champion while Macrae combined his political principles with his acting talents, opening a briefcase which contained material allegedly relevant and commenting on its contents hilariously. He ended by telling his audience that he had been given a song written by an inmate of what now would be called by some name less pejorative and unfeeling than "Asylum" which was the word he used. The song with which he then favoured the company, told the story of a sparrow, shot at by a boy with a bow and arrow. The bird then few off leaving the arrow to strike a man hurling a barrow. And so on. This turn went down very well, and the song went on to meet fame in later TV programmes.

We collected donations to a limited extent, and spent much more than we received, especially on published propaganda. A recently founded student newspaper, the "Gilmorehill Guardian" was edited by Winnie O'Hara, and she undertook to produce for us a magazine called "A Cross for MacCormick". We had forgotten that voting at elections did not involve putting a cross on a ballot paper, but it made a snappy title, so we ignored the attempts by the Tories to make us better informed.

Another student paper, very much more militant and provocative than the Guardian, was the significantly named "Gilmorehill Girn". This was the work of Ian Hamilton, and his paper became highly popular and widely circulated among students. Its popularity was not however, universal, as some of Ian's targets took serious umbrage, and there was some talk of physical retribution. While this feud rumbled on, Ian produced for us "The Blue Bunnet" on lines similar to "Girn" but dealing specifically with Rectorial developments. His satirical skills brought an increase in the number of his ill-wishers, and he spent some time in the unidentified safe house which was my digs in 41 Oakfield Avenue.

The final event of any Rectorial campaign was the "Fight" – a battle arising as the supporters of one candidate fought to prevent all others from entering the polling place. Taking advantage of their shared accommodation the inmates of the Halls of Residence arrived early and blocked the doors in the interests of their candidate, Lord Inverchapel. Supporters of Dr George McLeod, the Labour candidate, were above such loutish behaviour, and only a few Tories turned up to protect the prospects of Sir David Maxwell Fyfe. Only the Covenant partisans spent a painful hour or two trying to break the Maclay Hall blockade. Those defenders were particularly quarrelsome because during the night before some miscreants had raided Maclay Hall and left MacCormick partisan signs to claim and admit their responsibility.

The rules were, that the fighting must end eventually to allow the less pugilistic students – women for instance – to cast their votes. Victory in a Rectorial required the candidate to win a majority of the Four Nations into which students from the various parts of Scotland were arranged. The Highlands and Islands were "Transforthana". Glasgow and its hinterlands was "Glottiana". The South East, and the rest of the world which sent students to Glasgow was "Loudoniana" and the South West was "Rotheseiana". We knew that Loudoniana was safe for Inverchapel, and we feared for our prospects, especially among women students, from the more genteel shires and country towns of the south west, but we hoped for the North and Glasgow to rally. That is how it worked out. In one of our songs we had envisaged the moment when

26

"From the balcony, Hector announces with glee
King John is the Rector for you and for me".

Glee was furthest of all emotions from the mind of Principal Sir Hector Hetherington, as
with clear regret he had to confirm the election of a man representing a cause which he
came nowhere near to understanding, and which he thus detested.

To the pleasure of success was added the relief when victory prompted donors to give us
the means to pay our campaign bills!

The Rectorial campaign had several consequences. As a result of our success, four of us
were co-opted on to the National Covenant Committee, Ron Fraser and Billy Craig for
the Liberals, and Ian Hamilton and myself for GUSNA. Craig was a major figure in
student society, Secretary and President of the Union, a splendid orator and a highly
capable young man. He became in due course Treasurer of the Liberal Party in Scotland,
and was deeply and genuinely an interpreter of Liberal principles, unlike others for whom
that party was just a convenient half-way house occupied as elections came and went by
those who were too guilty in their comfort to be Tories and too socially polished to fit
comfortably into local Labour parties.

Ian's "Blue Bunnet" had been a truly memorable part of our campaign, and had captured
the support and admiration of the new Rector. We drove King John on our open lorry
through Glasgow's West End to show our sense of triumph and happiness. "You know
James", he remarked as we passed along Sauchiehall Street, "I didn't do this for myself.
I did it for Scotland." I knew that was true, but I was perhaps ill-advised to agree so
readily in replying, "That's all right. So did we."

Attending the Covenant Committee I found pretty well what I had expected. Its members
were all men of standing and success in their professions. Their attachment to the Home
Rule cause was an enthusiasm, entirely genuine in most cases, but really an optional extra

in their lives, filling their leisure moments with purpose. In no way could these men ever have been expected to allow themselves to be subsumed in a party political organisation. They were there on a basis of principle arrived at by thinking for themselves, and remaining as members very much as equals and on their own terms.

Some of them by now I knew. Bertie Gray, always cheerful and decent, and Dewar Gibb, Scots Law Professor, a familiar figure to Glasgow students for years, who had, like Bertie, followed MacCormick, out of the SNP of which he had once been Chairman. Nigel Tranter perhaps the most successful Scottish novelist of his time, Neville Davidson, Minister of Glasgow's Cathedral, John J. Campbell and John Bayne, prominent Glasgow lawyers and influential Catholic laymen, Bayne at least being an open Labour sympathiser. Presumably sharing his views was Michael Byrne of the Scottish Horse and Motormen's Union, who was expected to pass on the wishes and expectations of organised labour. Three of us sat quietly but Billy participated vigorously and confidently in various discussions. Meetings passed, interesting rather than invigorating. Change was not long delayed.

Some time in the spring of 1951 I met by chance as it seemed with Ian Hamilton and Bob Shirley as they came up the steps in to the Arts quadrangle. We stopped and exchanged whatever news we had and then Ian revealed that he had a plan. He was going to attempt to remove the Stone of Destiny from Westminster Abbey and turn its release to great popular political advantage. The sensational possibilities were obvious to anyone with half a sense of political emotion, and the sheer bold ambition of the idea was barely to be comprehended on this first hearing. He was forming a team to carry through the plan he said, and would I care to join? Then, and forever, I was and remained moved by the invitation, but I could not begin to credit the possibility of success. Still, it would be a marvellous publicity triumph. Who else, I asked, did he propose to involve? Well, Billy Craig he replied. I have felt remorse ever since over the churlish response which was to the effect that I could not with confidence enter into a joint enterprise with Billy.

I was wrong, and my remorse springs from this expression of distrust in Billy. I can only plead that I spoke before hindsight. Billy Craig was just too successful, too authoritative, too confident, altogether too at home in circles like the Covenant Committee. To imagine him participating with serious discretion in a student venture like Ian's did not ring true. As events were to show I was quite mistaken, as I have admitted to Ian since. But I didn't join, and regret for my decision is added to my remorse over my misjudging of Billy.

So, without me, the expedition went ahead. A few days before Christmas I met Ian in Sauchiehall Street carrying a large thin package whose open end revealed a crowbar. It was his father's, he explained. Was he in the burglar trade? I asked, and we went our ways. So the events over Christmas inevitably came as no surprise to me.

The consequences were largely as might have been expected. Only a few socially uptight groups of starched Scots shared the alleged shock of the state's spokespersons. Most ordinary people indicated delight, let alone support. As the University's Fifth Centenary torchlight procession made its way along the city streets towards the University, our GUSNA banner was cheered and much happy comment followed us. I used to claim in later years that if the SNP had then had anything like the membership which it later attained, the strength of feeling on display would have driven the cause forward some 30 years earlier than any prospect of success could be glimpsed.

There was some practical political benefit. The Convenant or rather John MacCormick and a few close associates, organised tours of the country using the liberation of the Stone as an occasion for evangelism.

My share in this touring campaign was to speak at several towns in Ayrshire and finally, to my great pleasure, in Greenock. The hall in the Temperance Institute in West Stewart Street where Sam Shields was custodian, was not large enough to accommodate the audience, and smaller rooms were pressed into service to deal with the overflow. It was at this meeting that I first discovered that there had grown up the custom of having the

29

audience sing the 23rd Psalm to start proceedings. I felt it fitted with the prevailing fervour of the moment, but there were other opinions.

At the next meeting of the National Committee, psalm singing was criticised by John Bayne and John J. Campbell, who took exception to such a display of Presbyterian tradition as being likely to give offence to Catholics. No argument followed and the practice was dropped as far as I was aware.

Dissensions were, however, beginning to appear in the Covenant ranks. I was neither surprised nor distressed by such signs. The whole all-party, no-party, come-all-ye posture of the Covenant always seemed to me, as to anyone favouring political discipline and organisation, a silly basis on which proper planning was never going to succeed. Divisions were always going to exist unmodified, and, with no discipline enforced by a constitution, or by the withholding of patronage, they would always in due course be revealed and expressed.

At a mass national demonstration in Glasgow's St Andrew's Hall, this fact was made very clear. On the platform with John MacCormick were the Duke of Montrose, and, as speakers Sheriff John Bayne and Professor Dewar Gibb. MacCormick was his usual impressive oratorical self. The Duke was then given the task of introducing, for money-raising purposes, Covenant Bonds, to be sold and redeemed following the election of a Scottish government. Again a movement wholly voluntary was never going to be easily persuaded to offer such material support, but the Duke set the best example he could, and pledges were offered from the audience. All was well thus far.

When John Bayne spoke he explained that we were all united in our cause and had set aside our party loyalties. However, he had to say that he felt that Churchill and his Conservative party deserved no support from anyone who remembered their party's years in pre-war governments. A grey-haired but agile man a few rows in front of where Jarvis and I were sitting arose with shaking fist and claimed that Bayne was "against Churchill because he wanted to take control of the ports from your treacherous Irish friends."

To restore harmony it fell to Dewar Gibb. He too had put aside all petty party loyalties and was entirely committed to the broadest principles of unity. He did, however, feel that he must point out that Mr Churchill was devotedly serving his country while the leaders of the Labour Party were "skulking behind prison bars."

It made for a memorable evening. What MacCormick must have made of it one can guess. Punishment by press publicity was surprisingly lenient and reflecting on having got away with the debacle reasonably unscathed, Jarvis remarked "Scots of all parties, unite! You have nothing to lose but your bonds."

The rescuing of the Stone of Destiny had been a tremendous stimulus to Scottish National sentiment and to the Covenant and campaigning. In due course however a decision had had to be taken as to its future. Ian Hamilton and John MacCormick have both written their account of the reasons for returning the Stone to the custody of the state. I later was advised that the illness of King George and his personal distress weighed heavily upon all who had to decide. To be found hiding the Stone on the day the King died would be as much of a political disaster as its original release had been a political triumph. So its return, in retrospect, was always on the cards. MacCormick has told us how he expected some degree of tact and seemly dignity from the government. No doubt he should have known better, but that is hardly a fault.

There were, however, those of us who were enraged by the callous tactics of the police and whoever was instructing them. To call it "scant ceremony" would be an exaggeration. With no ceremony at all but in loutish and brutal fashion, the Stone was hustled by the police from Arbroath Abbey and lodged in Forfar police custody. So at least was reported in Glasgow in the afternoon of 11th April 1951. By that evening a posse had been organised to go to Forfar and rescue it again.

In Glasgow's Buchanan Street station on the last train to Aberdeen there mustered a dozen of us, veterans of the Rectorial campaign. Flitting about at the barrier, and later boarding the train, were various private individuals, some recognisable to us. One was Wendy Wood, famous Nationalist publicist, whose exploits were usually so at variance with political cunning as to be counter-productive. Wendy did, as we all appreciated, have a keen desire to cause trouble for the authorities when they offered affront to Scotland. That night she saw some potential in the mood and she paid the fares for twelve students to be carried to Forfar.

Once on board Wendy sat somewhere with her own people. In our compartment we were joined by the journalist David Murray, a man who always seemed about to lose his temper and thus seemed usually bitter and confrontational in speech. His theme was broadly speaking, the perfidy of John MacCormick in surrendering the Stone. In an emotional state we were not really inclined to argue. On reaching Perth the train was to sit for a few minutes. The poet Morris Blythman, pen name Thurso Berwick, appeared and announced his intention to phone Nationalists in Perth and ask for their support. He returned looking rather bemused and explained that Perth couldn't help because they were having a jumble sale tomorrow. So, without reinforcements, we reached Forfar and made for the police station. Whether there was a sergeant and a constable or just one officer was not clear. No physical obstruction was offered as our vanguard looked into cells and behind the desk, shouting back "It's no here." So with failure our lot we had to work out how to get from Forfar to Glasgow at something like 3 o'clock in the morning. From somewhere came the suggestion that we could join a milk train which came through Perth at 4 or thereabouts. All very well, but how to get to Perth?

At this point there came forward a helpful little man in a camel coat, who presented himself as a reporter from the Scottish Daily Mail. Taxis were beyond our means, but we had heard tales of journalists' expenses, so we believed him when he offered to summon taxis to take us to Perth. We were thus able to reach Perth, join the milk train and return to Glasgow. Some optimists who felt that all was not lost got hold of the rumour that the Stone was being driven south in a police car and so a select few set off in a small car – a Ford Anglia as I recall – to pursue a police Jaguar or some such to set up an ambush at Abington. And that didn't work either.

As we all dispersed at the station, our press benefactor was full of praise for us. What a marvellous bunch of lads we were and how impressed by our commitment he was. We must at all costs keep in touch, and he was sure he could be of help in the future.

A few days later I was paged in the Glasgow University Union to take a call, which turned out to be from our friend Reg. Once again he lavished praise, and invited me urgently to meet him in the Spanish Lounge of the Royal restaurant at the foot of West Nile Street. He had some suggestions that he wanted to talk over.

In response, I called on Jarvis and together we went to the Lounge, where, true to his word, Reg was waiting. He had given his recent experiences a lot of thought, he explained, and had reached the belief that we were really the kind of admirable young men who would do whatever could be done to further Scottish liberation. Was he right? We gave some modest vague sounds of agreement and invited him to suggest what sort of things he had in mind. Well, it emerged, he really felt that we could best serve Scotland's interests by blowing up the bridges, road & rail both apparently, at Berwick.

To mull over this proposal we hastened back to my room and there conferred with Alasdair Macdonald, our GUSNA colleague. Alasdair had a great circle of professionally informed and qualified contacts and he undertook to take soundings as to the lunacy of the proposal before us. Back came the advice that any such attempt would leave a dirty black mark on the otherwise unscathed bridges, but might likely blow off a hand, and perhaps a head.

With this insight we returned to report to Reg. We asked if he could perhaps give some more specific advice. How would we get the explosives for instance? The answer seemed vague, but some power, somehow, would provide. How then would we set about the work? Well, just wire the gelignite to the uprights of the bridge. How do we get it to that point? On some sort of raft. And how do we get the raft there? Swim, pushing it in front of you. I can't swim I confessed sadly. He was obviously now viewing me with increasing displeasure, and it seemed time to draw the meeting to a close. I told him of Alasdair's report and said that there the matter ended. I said that I couldn't decide if he was just looking for a scoop to please his editor, or a crime to please the security agents of the state. Either way, we didn't want to see him again, and we never did.

A year later, four students were jailed for a year for agreeing, under the prompting of a taxi driver, a special constable in his spare time, to blow up the Post Office in Edinburgh. I phoned the Mail's office in Glasgow, and no-one had heard of our Reg. I heard later that he had gone to South Africa where his skills might well have been in demand. Jarvis and Alasdair are both gone now, and corroboration, or lack of it, worried me. However, I have learned that Alasdair had made his sister aware of the whole episode and so I have some measure of evidential support if ever required to provide it.

Given these four hectic years of activity in the Nationalist cause, my academic career, which had got off to an excellent start, had suffered from neglect. During the Rectorial campaign, I was tipped off by Esmond Wright of the History Department that the Professor, Andrew Browning, was beginning to show concerned displeasure over my absences. It would be polite, Esmond advised, if I called upon the Professor to seek his tolerance.

I made an appointment and duly presented myself at his door. Without looking up from his desk he greeted me, "Ah! Mr Halliday. I though you were dead." Then looking up he continued, "You're not dead, are you?" Andrew Browning's mind was razor sharp, and his temper matched, so I was much relieved when nothing more was said of my neglect of academic duty.

My wickedness had taken its toll however, as I found when I went for a tutorial on a major piece of work in my final year, to Douglas Chandaman, who had been my lecturer in both first and final years. Having enjoyed his good opinion in the early days, I was much shaken by his chilly greeting, "What on earth has happened to you?" Then my various short-comings were examined and deplored while I wondered how far I could ever regain any measure of approval from the History Department which I so greatly admired and respected.

After a fashion I did, graduating with reasonable approval in 1952. I came under Douglas Chandaman's supervision some 10 years later when he encouraged me in research studies and postgraduate recognition.

But the great student days were over, and how quickly we felt out of touch. While at Jordanhill during teacher training, I was recalled to speak for GUSNA and was expected to perform as acceptably as in the past. Unfortunately my performance was disastrous, a humiliation for me and a disappointment to the new generation in the Club. Shame prevented me from ever again standing on the debating floor, over which I had once presided. It appeared therefore that I was now back in the humblest of all categories, the new entrant to a profession, having to learn new skills and start from scratch all over again. The old wartime phrases thrown at new recruits by their more experienced elders came sharply back to mind. "Get some in" they would say. "Get your knees brown." Great antidotes to presumption and impertinent assertiveness from the inexperienced.

However, some memory of happier times lingered in some minds, and brought me back into the political arena.

One young man who joined GUSNA towards the end of my time in the Club was Ninian Gibson. Ninian was the son of Tom Gibson, President of the SNP, a Nationalist pioneer and stalwart from the days even before the formation of the National Party of Scotland. Tom had been a leader in the Scots National League, the body whose principles and strategic ideas provided the foundations of the later policies and practices of the SNP. Ninian's mother, a Nationalist pioneer and heroine in her own right, was Elma Campbell, who had fought Parliamentary elections in the early '30s. Ninian had obviously good genes, and excellent examples from his earliest days, and he had proved an excellent reinforcement to GUSNA's ranks.

Out of the blue in 1954 I received a letter from Ninian. He told me that the SNP were considering nominating a candidate to contest the next General Election in Stirling and Falkirk Burghs Constituency, which included Grangemouth as well as the two named burghs. The constituency had been contested at a by-election with the sort of result which was all one could expect or hope for at the time.

I had just started work. The only money I had was that month's pay cheque, and I had already learned that the warning of an experienced colleague in my first staff room was all too true. All teachers he said suffered because their pay was retrospective, not paid in advance. You will never make up that month he predicted, and he was right. However, and with shame I have to admit, I was flattered by Ninian's belief that I was, in his opinion, a fit person to be thought of as a candidate.

Some contemporaries in the Union had been parliamentary candidates. Dick Mabon had stood in my then home constituency of Bute and North Ayrshire. By chance when my family home moved to West Renfrewshire, so did Dick, prior to his selection and eventual election for Greenock. With obviously less prospect of success, my old Rectorial colleague, Ron Fraser, had been Liberal candidate and the youngest contestant in Scotland, in Govan.

My election experience was negligible. Alasdair and I had spent some time helping in Robert McIntyre's campaign in Motherwell in 1950, but in 1951, when Robert had moved to Perth, I was not active outwith the University.

I learned subsequently, what I have come to see as my greatest service to the Party, that Robert, facing the prospect of having to fight Perth as the sole SNP candidate in the country, had indicated that unless he found someone to stand beside him, he would feel moved to give up the fight which no-one else seemed ready to join. For good or ill I knew nothing of this at the time, and agreed to go through to meeting the Stirling CA officials in the Douglas Hotel in Stirling.

CHAPTER 3

ENTERING INTO THE WORK OF THE PARTY: 1955-6

Some personal doubts had to be resolved before I felt able to accept the role of "prospective candidate". I was arranging to marry in July 1955, only a few months ahead. I had changed jobs, having left Further Education in Ardeer and entered Kildonan Secondary School in Coatbridge, where, as the most recently appointed members of staff in a new post always find, they have to work out their own role. In the meantime, I was facing another hospital experience, as the old abdominal wound from my peritonitis adventure was requiring to be dealt with.

Then there was the matter of continuing to earn my living. Local authorities may, for all I know, have offered varying conditions to employees seeking election to Parliament, and asking for time off work to allow them to do so. Very possibly, more supportive deals were on offer elsewhere, to others, but I was told that Lanarkshire would allow only unpaid leave of absence. The Constituency Association agreed to pay three weeks' rent for the flat which I was preparing to move into and, as for living costs in the meantime, I was assumed to be able to cope.

As well as these personal arrangements there was a remaining political courtesy to be considered. The Covenant Association by 1954 was very much less in evidence than formerly. At the last meeting of its National Committee which I attended, a very outspoken attack had been made upon MacCormick and Ian Hamilton by David Murray. If he had confined himself to argument about tactics, he might have earned some support, but he allowed himself to question the motives of both men in their handing back of the Stone, insinuating that they had derived financial or professional advantage from arranging its return. Making his response John MacCormick showed anger for the only time I ever saw him do so.

Though the Covenant seemed to be resting, I felt I owed it to King John to let him know what had happened between me and the SNP. We met in a lounge in Woodlands Road, and he listened to my story. His response was very significant. "Hold off just now, if you can", he said. "The Covenant will very soon be announcing that it will contest elections, and will be choosing its candidates." I never knew, from that day to this, how much discussion had taken place, and how far, and how many, of his colleagues were in favour of the reversal of the reasoning which underlay the creation of the Convention and which since 1942, had been the fundamental difference of principle between it and the SNP. It may well be that he had discussed it with Ian Hamilton, his closest associate by this time. If he did, then Ian and I are the only people who know that this plan was in MacCormick's mind. If he kept it secret, even from Ian, then I am alone in possession of this nugget of political information.

I thought things over, rather briefly I admit, and then gave Stirling C.A. my consent to meet and consider my nomination.

At that first ever meeting I met the people who were to be my political colleagues, supporters and friends over the next two General Elections, and, on a personal basis, friends for as long as we co-existed.

In the Chair was Robert Porteous from Grangemouth. Bob was enormously respected in Grangemouth, where he was known for his service to youth organisations, and for his expert knowledge of the local area and its history. He was an admirable leader, always calm and sensible, and full of good campaigning ideas. His Grangemouth colleagues were, it seemed, from the late 30 or early 40 age group, very much ordinary, sensible friends and neighbours within their town.

The Chairman of Stirling Branch, James Ellis, was one of a group of young men who had become politically active under the wing of Robert Curran who had been the Party's candidate in the constituency in the by-election of 1948. His colleagues included Robert Campbell, who has gone on to enjoy the life-long experience of service to the Party.

38

Sitting slightly apart and looking like a man who wouldn't much care for pointless blethers, was Murdoch Young. I spoke, to explain myself and my outlook on things, answered a few questions, and went back home to wait for whatever the response would be. It came in a letter from Bob, written on the same evening, telling me that they wanted me to be their candidate. So, I went back for another meeting to plan ahead. Firstly I had to warn that I would be out of action at some stage because of surgery. We just had to hope that the timing of the election would suit me. Then they asked if I had any person in mind to act as Election Agent, and I asked if Murdoch Young would take it on. My wish was, it seemed, just what the C.A. would have wished, and so Murdo and I joined in an alliance which lasted through two elections and beyond until his death. He had been a founder member of the National Party in 1928, and his loyalty and total trustworthiness had continued unbroken since.

Our planning then turned to publicity. Leaflets and posters and the like were needed. It was Robert Campbell who had the idea that we might give colourful evidence of our loyalty by combining the ground colours of Scotland's two flags, the blue of the Saltire and the gold of the Lion Standard. Combining them, Robert thought, would mean blue lettering on a golden-yellow background. In due course posters to Robert's specifications were produced. The yellow-gold was fine, but the blue came out as black. What was to be done?

What I did not mention then or afterwards, was that I had a quite irrational sentimental liking for black and gold. In 1954 I had two reasons for this affection – Glasgow University was one and Glasgow's black and gold were linked to the happy years of my youth just passing away! The other was Melrose Rugby Club, which I used to visit annually, enjoying the local connections of my aunt. So, rather than abandon Robert's idea I snatched at it, and in a way prevented any further argument by getting my aunt to make black and gold rosettes, one for Murdo and one for me. These are the first rosettes, certainly in the post-war years, ever used by SNP campaigners. The Party had not felt any need for rosettes. When the matter was briefly mentioned one day in Alex Meikle's house in Falkirk, Alex, who had looked on Robert Curran as an honorary son, thought that a tartan buttonhole would do. However, as an early supporter of putting aside tartan imagery, I talked long and confusingly enough to divert Alex.

Purely personal sentiment was further encouraged when I went to work first in Uddingston Grammar School and then in Dunfermline High, both of which had black and gold as their colours.

In later years when I came to realise that personal animosities could distort judgement on many wholly irrelevant and pointless issues, I was glad that I had kept my personal motives secret. Whether prompted by gender, or a feeling of warmth for the colour of the thistle and the heather, was never made clear, but each in her turn, Margo MacDonald and Isobel Lindsay sought to attach pinkish-mauve stickers to the Party's publicity. The changes took for a little while, but the black and gold made its comeback, and I enjoyed seeing men of such eminence, and of such very divergent opinions, as Douglas Henderson and Alex Salmond wearing black and gold rosettes in due course.

The whole argument provided Donald Stewart with one of his better leg-pulls. He would leak a hint that a split threatened to distract the Party. When his excited victims began to speculate on what the row might be about, he would reveal that rival factions had formed, favouring one colour over the other. He worked the same trick on another occasions, suggesting with a worried, straight face, that the rival feelings over the Saltire and the Lion Rampant could not for much longer be kept in control.

At the meeting when my nomination was confirmed I met with a man who seemed to know most people present, some of them greeting him with a sort of deference. Murdo on the other hand, I noticed, gave him no such consideration. I wondered what the story was. It emerged that this was the Editor of the "Scots Independent", a Major James Glendinning. I have never warmed to Nationalists who see fit to hold on to British Military titles, even in cases where I know they are otherwise good people. Glendinning I didn't know.

We spoke, and in confident, measured tones he told me that he might have been selected for Stirling but had pretty well committed himself to Greenock. I made some silly jest about swapping pulpits, and there the matter rested. The background to Murdo's behaviour became clear whenever the election was over.

The actual campaign of 1955 was happy. It began in very low-key fashion, because a newspaper strike destroyed the chance for any grief-stricken farewell to Churchill by the Tories. The succession of Anthony Eden was never heralded with headlines and public comment because nothing was appearing in print. So, anyhow, Churchill was gone and the most glamorous of all his political generation, Eden, now followed him into office. The new man, it was expected, would win the election, and so it turned out.

The Constituency officials had prepared a competent campaign plan. The one snag was transport. None of us had a car, and times and distances involved in getting around within and between Stirling, Falkirk and Grangemouth by bus proved very wasteful of energy, time and costs. But we did our best. We would arrange as many of a day's events as possible within the one town. We'd visit homes in the mornings, and arrange work place meetings in canteens or at factory gates during workers' lunch hours. On each evening we'd have a public meeting in one or other municipal ward, in a school or similar public building.

Never once did I meet any hostility. Audiences varied, never very large, but only once really sparse. Supporting speakers from the Party and the University too, came along to put their opinions on our behalf.

As well as these ward meetings we had a kind of set piece Rally-type meeting in major halls. The Albert Hall was the venue in Stirling, and the Town Halls in Falkirk and Grangemouth saw our audience addressed by the Party's top brass and best known personalities. Tom Gibson and Arthur Donaldson, Alex Aitken and Frank Yeaman, Blair Wilkie and Oliver Brown all spoke, often to gratifyingly large audiences.

41

The Local papers in 1955 were plentiful. Stirling had the "Observer", the "Journal" and the "Sentinel". Falkirk had its "Herald", "Sentinel" and "Mail" and Grangemouth, covered by the "Herald", also had its "Sentinel" and "Advertiser". The reporters from all papers were wholly pleasant, and some even would call me at night with tip-offs about the evening. The editor of the "Journal", Donald Cameron, was a supporter and adviser, and a very great help then and in the years which followed. All the signs were encouraging, but, of course, within the limits imposed by the fact that we were puny souls in comparison with the main parties. Our only wistful hope was that we might do well enough to save our deposit by gaining over an eighth of the votes. Our last total at the by-election was well short of what was needed. In an electorate of about 50,000, a target of about 6,000 was a lot of people. In more recent times with a target of a twentieth or 5%, we'd have had no bother. But that was then, and we lost our £150.

The campaign ended with some innocent fun at the vote count. Candidates and agents were invited as a courtesy to meet with the Returning Officer in his room. When it was our turn to enter, the Returning Officer, the elderly Sheriff Maconochie, raised his head from the portable radio by his ear, and, with pleased excitement said, "We've had three gains so far. Ah, the Conservatives I should say have had three gains." His depute, Sheriff Murray, stood statue-like. Sheriff Maconochie wasn't finished with us. We had to go in again, all three candidates and agents, to see and agree upon the voting papers set aside as questionable. Where a cross should have been marked in a box after the candidate's name, some voters had put some other symbol. We lost one vote because someone over-enthusiastic had drawn a thistle. Some, instead of putting a cross in the proper box, had put a cross through the candidate's name. It could be argued that that wasn't meant to be a vote, but was rather an attempt to put the evil eye on the candidate. Then there were those who instead of a cross, put 1, 2 and 3 opposite the names. Others put 1, 2 and X, obviously with football pools in mind. Even more peculiar than being guided by football pools, were those whose behaviour was conditioned by raffles. They had filled in their cross but had torn their ballot paper in four and popped the pieces into the box.

These four pieces were found, reassembled, and assessed by us standing around. It was agreed that the voter's intentions were clear so the pieces were stuck together with Sellotape, and the vote was solemnly counted.

Having observed all these misdeeds the Sheriff felt moved to comment. As most idiocies had involved votes intended for Labour, he smiled kindly upon the Labour candidate and said, "I think many of your voters have been drunk today, Mr McPherson." With some self control Malcolm McPherson looked at him, whereupon, unwilling to let well alone, the Sheriff said, "Perhaps that's why they voted for you."

Polling management on any election day has a habit of providing comedy; Stirling in 1955 was a really top-class occasion.

On the following day, Murdo and I got the train to Perth to meet with Robert McIntyre and Perth's most influential SNP official, Malcolm Shaw. Robert had secured a very good vote again in Perth which he had already contested in 1951. At this meeting I first became aware of an ongoing crisis within the Party, which was coming to a head over developments concerning the "Scots Independent". The paper was supervised by an editorial Board of six, three from the SNP and three from the Scots Secretariat, Mr Muirhead's organisation. This board had appointed James Glendinning as editor.

It might have been a matter of principle. It most certainly was a matter of proper concern for the good opinion of the electorate. At all events, one of the many destructive and widely-believed charges against the SNP was that it encouraged and relied upon anti-English emotion and prejudice. It is a charge, as everyone knows, used day and daily by our opponents, and in these days, having just emerged from a war infected with racial hatreds, the Party had to disavow Anglophobia and certainly put a stop to any which actually might exist.

The S.I. in the view of the SNP members of its Board, Robert McIntyre, John Smart, National Secretary, and Malcolm Shaw, had given signs of readiness to use Anglophobia in presenting our case.

There were reports coming from experienced SNP people in Edinburgh that the Edinburgh University Scottish Nationalist Club was voicing racist comments against the English as such, rather than solely against a government responsive only to English voters. With little difficulty evidence came regularly in to the Party's Executive and thence to the S.I. Board. Rabble-rousing speeches at the Mound might entertain many who hung around to enjoy the fun, but from any serious political standpoint the Party's reputation for political common sense, decency and integrity would be put at risk.

Then copies of a typed and copied political journal called "The Nationalist" came to hand. At an early stage I was given copies of a dozen or so editions for me to read and make up my mind. There was a lot which was pretty run-of-the-mill Nationalist argument, but there were some odd and needless references to various overseas bodies of no relevance that one could see. Much attention was lavished upon the Ukrainian underground. In our own time, politics in the Ukraine would interest very few, but in 1955 memories were all too fresh of Ukrainian collaboration with the Nazis. People looked then with horror on Nazi connections, no matter that people now are readier to research motives for such behaviour.

These papers seemed rather ill-judged, and then I found an issue about propaganda, and an article which was all too familiar. I checked and confirmed that it was a verbatim lift of a passage from Hitler's "Mein Kampf", in which the Nazi leader explained his attitude towards publicity. Ordinary people, he explained, were dull-witted, so, for them, propaganda must be reduced to simple slogans, repeated again and again. "The Nationalist" was quite openly the work and brainchild of Mr Glendinning, and our three Board members felt it wrong that the S.I. should be left in his editorial hands.

When the Board met, the SNP side moved to end Mr Glendinning's tenure as editor of the S.I. This was opposed by the other three, but carried by Robert McIntyre's casting vote as Chairman.

This was probably the first time I had occasion to notice how persons of wildly contrasting and, indeed, conflicting, political views could put these differences aside and joyously unite in attacking the SNP. Mr Muirhead, who had had a long connection with the S.I., and whose brother had been a consistent supporter of the paper, now took several steps to do what he could to damage it. His political attitudes throughout his career had always placed him on the side of minimal discipline and party organisation. He had a long-standing history of arguments with a Party disciplinarian par excellence like Tom Gibson; with an official of the day who took a similar view, Malcolm Shaw; and, often reluctant, but as the Party's Organiser in the troubled days of 1942, a man who opposed internal lawlessness, Robert McIntyre.

Joining Mr Muirhead was Robert Blair Wilkie whose dislike of Robert McIntyre was beyond explanation or probability. After Robert had been elected M.P. for Motherwell, he returned to attend the next meeting of the National Council. He used to remember sadly, that expecting a good reception he was instead fiercely attacked by Wilkie for "coming here with your Westminster ways". On occasions in later years he would refer to "the egregious Dr McIntyre". What lay behind all this I was never able to find out, and I was always too embarrassed to ask Wilkie for his reasons.

The third Secretariat Board member was Stirling business-man, by then retired, Harry Barr. Mr Barr had a good name with Stirling Branch. He had given good support to Robert Curran and probably, though I never knew any details, had given a financial helping hand from time to time. Like other men of his background whom I have met over the years, he was perhaps too quickly impressed by the brisk certainties of men of authoritarian political habits.

However it was not Harry Barr but his brother who left me struggling to explain some things to him. Hearing me ask that we should all reject Anglophobia, he argued that Mr Glendinning had merely been exercising "vigorous criticism". He could not then, and probably never could , understand that we can "vigorously criticise" anyone for his opinions, his deeds or his behaviour, but we are wrong and ridiculous if we argue that we can "vigorously criticise" anyone for something he can't help, notably his nationality.

So the S.I. lost Mr Muirhead's financial goodwill, possibly Mr Barr's and any civility from Mr Wilkie. Mr Glendinning turned to his base in Edinburgh, and organised a formidable faction seeking to take control of the Party.

At the National Conference, lines were drawn and rival slates of candidates confronted one another. The "rebel" group called itself the "55 Group"; published a Conference bulletin, and campaigned all through the Conference highways and byways for support.

Tom Gibson as President was opposed by Sam Shields from Greenock. Sam was a bluff, apparently cheerful man who was capable of some very telling and very vicious arguments when he chose. To oppose Robert McIntyre as Chairman, James Glendinning put himself in the ring. Other offices were contested except, as I recall, National Treasurer, a thankless job requiring real work and a real degree of intelligence. In any case the position was held by David Rollo, who was viewed with genuine affection by most and with tactful toleration even by the malcontents.

One cunning 55 Group stalwart believing himself to be unidentified, wrote to John Smart asking for delegate credentials even though he did not qualify. He admitted that this was so, but promised that all delegate cards which came his way would be used to ensure votes for Dr McIntyre and the "incumbent" nominees. Fortunately Robert and John were both sufficiently genuine in their adherence to the rules so this little piece of rascality did not succeed.

In the end, the "55 slate" was defeated, their one future defence and argument being that branches in Perth, where lay major and genuine SNP membership strength, had been recognised outwith the rules and Standing Orders. That story has never been formally renounced though largely forgotten.

The atmosphere in the conference hall was understandably very tense, excited and nasty, with a swift rush by various persons to settle matters "outside". Some removing of jackets and such preparations did occur, but mercifully came to nothing. No ringleader put himself at risk, though one lady, moved by partisan emotions, called for some of Mr Glendinning's young men to go to the support of those involved in the threatening exchanges. They either didn't hear, or didn't feel inclined to respond to her urgings. All of those prominent in these events are now dead, and I can only think of two who are still around.

The failure of the 55 Group to secure control of the Party and machinery left them to work over their next move. The successful incumbent faction equally had to consider how far a Party so riven by distrust and dislike could effectively function.

As has, in later years, been the case in the SNP, any recent Parliamentary candidate is sure of support in internal elections. As the only recent candidate, apart from our re-elected Chairman, I had been elected to the National Executive, where all decisions on how best to deal with disunity were now taken.

Basically, those who continued to promote words and deeds which the NEC considered to be electorally damaging, were to be asked to desist, with disciplinary action to be proposed if they refused. There was no ultimatum. All decisions were to be put into effect very gradually, with every opportunity for reconsideration. Principally the ruling was intended to stop the anti-English utterances which the gleeful Press were now reporting regularly from the Mound's soap boxes.

One sadly recurring feature of these internal disputes, is that those most heated in their discontent hold the leaders of the Party in such contempt that they take their cowardly failure to act for granted. It still happens. "Bumbling old fearties" is how one of the Proclaimers a few years ago described his targets, whoever they were. I presumed that I was one of them, though I had neither power nor office at the time when he was rendered so indignant.

So it was to be expected that the NEC warnings would be dismissed and defiance would follow. The National Council in September 1955 passed by 31 votes to 4 a motion declaring that racial hatred and the incitement of violence were contrary to the policy of the SNP. It was a calm enough, factual motion, giving every chance for reflection and acceptance. One influential voice speaking for last-minute reconciliation was that of Arthur Donaldson. The opportunity was not taken, and with much zest, and, if I judge his feelings correctly, glee, Douglas Henderson, the most impressive of Mr Glendinning's supporters, persevered in repeating his oratory, and was declared to have expelled himself by his behaviour.

In her recent thesis, which any who wish to learn more, would do well to read, Dr Paula Somerville has recorded what followed. She writes that "dozens" of Party members resigned, and gives some names. I think she exaggerates the numbers, because there were really very few "dozens" in the entire Party! She may possibly have come upon some of the 55 Group views, written or oral, consistently boasting of their strength, which in fact never proved itself to any real extent.

Some of the names I have forgotten. David Smith, Andrew Currie and Archie McPherson are still to the fore in their various positions and activities. If you do read Dr Somerville's thesis, please note that the Donald Stewart who was one of those who resigned, was not Donald Stewart of Stornoway, our future Party President, M.P. and Parliamentary Group leader, but another Donald Stewart, ex Provost of Doune, a lively, likeable man who had allowed himself to be talked into alliance with the others.

The main strength as was to be expected in a faction originating in Edinburgh University, was the city of Edinburgh. In that city there was the long-established Edinburgh Branch, whose members included people with life-long commitment to the Party and its cause. Frank Yeaman, a 1945 candidate, was Chairman. His colleagues included George Dott, thinker, writer and activist since the Party's earliest days, Mary Fraser, now Mary Dott, George's wife, and ex National Secretary; and Alex Aitken, sometime Party Treasurer, History teacher in the Royal High and in Trinity High, who had taught several of those who were now moved to ridicule him and his colleagues. No doubt they were "bumbling old fearties", though the phrase had not yet been coined.

In Edinburgh then, and no doubt elsewhere, as, for instance, in Dundee in the late 1960s, those at odds with their parent branch habitually went off and formed their own. If their strength was genuine and sufficient, they would then be able to claim recognition and function as a Branch with the approval of the NEC. In Edinburgh several such groups had mushroomed – "South", "West", "East" and "George Square". Whether their membership and funds were adequate to merit recognition was none too clear. Certainly Edinburgh Branch regarded them as branches on paper rather than in reality.

Individuals and their location I can recall as Dr Somerville states. She is a first-rate chronicler of the events which continued in 1955 and 1956, as the 55 Group re-created itself as the "Nationalist Party of Scotland" in truculent parody of the "National" Party, whose name had been deliberately chosen to emphasise its rejection of racist feelings and motives and they persevered in verbal violence and a few rather embarrassing leaflets, revealing all too obviously the over-excitable characteristics of adolescence.

Two practical reasons did help to bring the NPS into being and enable it to attract some support. Again, just as in 1942, impotence with lack of progress prompted anger, and the failure was too easily and unfairly attributed to the Party's leaders. The impatience was understandable, but to allow it to give rise to Fascist-type propaganda and behaviour was not. However, beyond the general discontent was the animosity which so many displayed towards Robert McIntyre in person. I never understood why such vicious emotions were so often revealed, and how hurtful it must have been to Robert I feel ashamed to imagine. But Robert himself, ever the servant of the Party, now decided that for the Party's good he had to step down.

CHAPTER 4

PARTY CHAIRMAN: 1956-60

Robert felt that he, personally, had become the issue, providing a pretext for discontented elements to spread discontent further. He believed that giving up the Chair would help to leave malcontents at a loss. His stepping down would, as the saying goes, shoot their fox. He may well have considered his older acquaintances and longer-serving colleagues, and he understandably discussed his plans with Tom Gibson and Arthur Donaldson. My recent election fight proved to be once again the seemingly obvious reason for advancement within the Party, and it was duly put to me that I should agree to take over the Chair. Knowing that several respected persons of experience would still be around, I consented.

I chaired my first Party Conference in the Allan Water Hotel in Bridge of Allan. A group photograph of those present was posed on the hotel steps. Significantly, there was plenty of room. There were some absentees who had gone off for lunch or something, but they were very few, and, looking at the photo, I could come very near to naming the absentees. That photo goes far to revealing the state of the Party in 1956.

The misery of the preceding year cast a lingering shadow over the company, and I wondered how they would react to me. My chances may not have improved when one of my first actions was to declare Mr Muirhead to be out of order when he, having spoken once on a motion under debate, rose to speak again. He was not alone in the SNP in assuming that orderly debate should be just like a conversation, as fluid and as inconclusive. I had decided that rules governing conduct of debate would be enforced, and though it was embarrassing that such a venerated figure as Mr Muirhead was made to toe the same line as everyone else, it had to be done. He did not participate in any future Party deliberations.

The Conference passed without any obvious damage, and I turned to dealing with the business of the NEC. For the next five years there was virtually no change in the membership of the NEC. Tom Gibson had been replaced as President by Robert McIntyre, but remained as an ordinary member. Vice-Chairmen were Malcolm Shaw of Perth and George Leask of Cambuslang. Secretary was John Smart of Glasgow, but with connections to Falkirk, and David Rollo of Kirkintilloch was Treasurer. Other members had specific functions. Finance Convener, hoping to find new ways to raise funds, was Willie Orr of Dumbarton. David Cathcart of Uddingston was S.I. Convener with the difficult job of persuading the Party to give serious thought to the provision of effective publicity, in particular making the S.I. as useful an instrument as it could be. This usually meant a recurring request for money, and David had the strength of will to confront those who grudged paying. Gordon Forsyth of Glasgow completed the elected line up. Others contributed by virtue of their activities in the wider Party. Alasdair MacDonald, my old colleague from GUSNA days, had edited the S.I. and had served as Finance Convener, so was a back-up to both Messrs Orr and Cathcart.

The Elmbank Street premises had been the Party's HQ for some years, initially made possible by support from the Muirhead brothers. During the troubles of 1954 and 1955, Mr Glendinning had been a frequent presence, but the office was now managed by Fiona Smart, wife of the National Secretary, and when Fiona decided to give her own domestic life a greater allocation of time, we were fortunate to have Mrs Angus as Office Manager. The premises were looked after by the residents Mr & Mrs Barclay, who were as well known to members as any of the NEC, and better liked perhaps than some.

I felt that my job was almost that of the US President on taking the oath – "to preserve, protect and defend the Constitution." Other words were in my mind as well as these. "Recover" was one. "Sustain" effort and "expand" activity and "reconcile" internally. All these had to be attempted as I began to assess the means at my disposal.

Everyone who has ever written about the SNP has had a shot at estimating its membership. The best informed and best qualified journalists and academics agree on a fairly low figure. They all have failed to understand quite how low.

The Constitution recognised, as a Branch, a body which could submit a list of 20 members minimum, and which could pay the fees due to HQ for that number. Methods of calculating the actual amounts which branches would incur varied from time to time, as branches tried to dodge, and David and Willie Orr tried to spot and block loopholes.

The essential fact is that in 1956 the branches which met constitutional requirements, genuinely, were Aberdeen, Dumbarton, Edinburgh, Hamilton, Kirkintilloch, Perth (several), Stirling, Grangemouth and Uddingston. Cambuslang was recognised but was really sustained by several supportive families. Forfar actually helped the Party out with a long-term loan, but its real activity was the influence and writing of Arthur Donaldson. In Falkirk we had a team which could show a presence at election time but not maintain a branch with an organised regular programme of activities.

What of the towns which could look back on Nationalist strength in past years. What of Motherwell? What of Alva? What of Arbroath? In places like that responsible volunteers had died, had moved on, had migrated or just grown tired. Arbroath had gone over to Convention and Covenant, and had never shown any notion of coming back.

In a whole list of places we had individuals who paid their dues directly to HQ. It can almost be read as a roll of honour. Wick, where the County Librarian held a lonely post for the Party, Stornoway where Donald Stewart was a known representative, Skye where Donald Cameron continued in the loyalty which he had adopted in his student days. Ayr had one known member, St Andrews and Kirriemuir likewise.

In comparison Dundee was a positive stronghold. It was home to Messrs Michie, McFarlane and Leslie and, under his "Sandy McIntosh" alias, Duncan Graham, and

Grace. Just appearing at a National Council in Perth was a new presence, Tom McFettridge.

In Glasgow the true state of affairs was hardly credible. Home Rule sentiment was weak in any case. Class and sectarian hatreds seemed to snuff out Scottish awareness, and such as there was had become diluted by being shared around with Convention/Covenant survivals, Scottish National Congress, the Scottish Patriots and the Nationalist Party of Scotland. Congress was in effect an extension of Mr Muirhead's Scots Secretariat, and was a proven refuge for anyone who had fallen out with the SNP strategy, SNP policies or SNP personalities. It also accommodated all who were drawn to various political novelties, even eccentricities. They were at pains to urge toleration for anyone who cared to profess broadly Home Rule sentiments, and treat all such as friends and comrades. It was with some grain of satisfaction that I heard news of a famous fracas in Bo'ness when these mutually tolerant enthusiasts were reportedly fighting along the pavement outside the pub from which they had been asked to move, punching and belabouring with briefcases. In due course the organisation was to test the Party's tolerance to destruction.

The Patriots were the followers of Wendy Wood, possibly the best known Nationalist name in the country. It is in keeping with the general lucklessness of our movement that the words and deeds of this famous lady were consistently exciting to those who had no intention of giving us their serious support, and consistently deterred many sober persons who might well have joined us had it not been that they were so well aware of Miss Wood's headlines.

The Nationalist Party had doubtless won over some SNP members, though it is difficult to be precise. One branch – Scotstoun – was reported to have joined, but that branch was their own creation with their own purposes in mind. It can hardly count as a defection of any significance.

What did matter was not defections, but a general poisoning of the whole Nationalist body throughout the city. Even if few had left the SNP, those who had not, and who

54

remained as members, behaved as if they had wanted to leave, might still consider doing so, and were irritable because they hadn't. There was a Glasgow West branch, of which I had become an alleged member, though I can recall no meeting ever being held. That may have been just as well, because I heard of meetings in previous times at which the business was to nominate the first Cabinet of an independent Scotland. The favoured Prime Minister was to be Mr Glendinning, while Dr McIntyre, in a commendable display of tolerance, was to be included as Minister of Health. This discussion took place at a time when there was hardly the numerical strength to canvass a Glasgow close, let alone a municipal ward or parliamentary constituency.

Another depressing report told of an unfortunate member who insisted on bringing to meetings all portable property, because, if not under constant personal supervision, it would be stolen by Lord Rothschild, who lurked by a street light across the road just waiting his chance to pounce.

This was a sad but not unique example of the unhappy personal problems which some members combined with their Nationalism. I was favoured with letters from several such in the next few years. If these incidents had been merely tragic afflictions of individuals we might all have been able to deal kindly with such embarrassments, but members sometimes would not allow this to happen. On more occasions than it bears thinking about, a person suffering from obvious inadequacies, would be nominated for office. Nominators perhaps didn't notice. Perhaps they took the view that it didn't matter. What was all too often true, was that those who knew perfectly well that there was a problem, were too embarrassed to point it out. It did happen to my own knowledge that the position of Press Officer was entrusted to a member whose literacy was frighteningly limited.

There was perhaps no smoothly functioning Glasgow West branch. What we did have was a number of honest, genuine Nationalists whose morale was shattered by the 55 Group and the NPS. Mr & Mrs John Stevenson and Mr and Mrs Cameron were the particular stalwarts. Also in membership was the Stevensons' son, Bobby, and Angus McIntosh, brother, as it turned out, of my old GUSNA friend, Hamish.

Mr & Mrs Stevenson, though often downcast, were always kind and courteous. Mr Cameron was a quiet sensible man and calm in his good manners. Mrs Cameron was another story. She was outraged on behalf of Mr Glendinning. She deeply disliked Dr McIntyre, and if guilt was to be shared around, she now, by extension, disliked me. Bobby was an alert, cheerful man, quite lively among us all but keeping his own counsel, certainly from me. Angus had an apparently infinite capacity for discontent, and a certainty that he had been betrayed somehow and would be again. There was nothing at all unacceptable in personal and political opinions of any of those fellow members, which makes their remorseless hostility to me all the more regrettable. I had no opening quarrel with them at all. They were in wait for me from the start. The only possible reason is that they were never going to see good in Robert McIntyre and they saw in me only an upstart pushed into office by him.

Before very long, however, a couple of discoveries brought about a change. Mrs Cameron discussed the war record of Mr Glendinning and the wounds which he had suffered, thus in her view removing any grounds for seeing Fascist characteristics in his public statements and actions. She reproached me for my unjust judgements and investigated my own past in her conversation. It then emerged that I had become a friend, while in hospital, of a fellow patient whom I held in high regard. This turned out to be Mr Cameron's nephew, whom they both held in great affection. With this common ground it now seemed that I wasn't such a bad fellow after all, and things became quite cordial.

The next crisis in my dealings with Glasgow SNP arose when a lively and determined lady, a teacher of History and a resident of Hillhead, had formed a contact with Angus. She was a Party member going back to the earliest days, and a survivor of several schisms and confrontations. She had been one of those who deplored the acceptance by the National Party of the merger with the Scottish Party – much to her credit in my view.

She was by temperament a close examiner and critic of any person in any position of authority, and Angus, taking Bobby along with him, decided to guide her into making trouble for me. I was Chairman, and therefore, by that definition, deserving to be humiliated if possible, and certainly exposed to embarrassment. Their chance came when I was to address a Glasgow rally in Hillhead Burgh Hall, and they brought along their new recruit. It was not clear at the time, and I certainly can't remember now, what I said to arouse her wrath. Whatever it was, she rose, a formidable presence, and wired into me on the grounds that, like me, she too was a teacher and "words do matter" in spite of my dismissive treatment of some topic. I could only stand and gape, having no idea of what I had done or said to annoy her. Angus's happiness was, as always, accompanied by an expression of doubt and disappointment. All out glee was never shown in my company at least. Bobby, however, sat with an ecstatic grin, relishing every second of my discomfiture. My ill-wishers had certainly dealt a most satisfying blow, and I expected more of the same to follow.

But it is often good policy to discuss, after a meeting with someone like this who had a grievance or criticism, what might be done to mend matters. I therefore stepped from the platform as she made her way to the door and asked if we could talk over her criticism. It still did not become clear. We never really reached that point, because we began by mutual introductions. She was Miss Phyllis Dorothea McCloskey, a Glasgow Honours graduate in History and a teacher of close on 30 years experience. She was now on the staff of Govan High School but had taught previously in the Glasgow High School for Girls. Was she by any chance teaching there at the relevant dates, I asked, and had she by any chance taught the girl who was now my wife? Her amazement was total and her conversion more or less immediate. She was militant in her championing of women's rights, so she had to be sure that I was more or less worthy of my wife, and once she concluded that this was so, I was wholly exonerated from whatever it was Angus had attributed to me.

Phyllis was a quite remarkable woman, a pioneer of women's rights and women's freedom of action. She had toured in the USSR in 1932 and had photos to prove it. She continued her travels after her retirement, visiting many countries, not only in Central Europe but Abyssinia, South Africa and Zambia, where she was in hospital with a broken leg. She was a most gallant and talented lady. Her sponsors had suggested to her that she might become SNP candidate for Hillhead, and they could hardly back down now. So I was delighted to support her adoption. She became a friend, even coping with visiting infants on occasions. She spoke for me, especially in Grangemouth where she was a great favourite. I became as helpful as possible as age and illness weakened everything but her marvellous pugnacious spirit. I served as her executor when the time came, and I have some of her art work in memoriam.

These difficulties arose in the West of Glasgow. In the East there was perhaps less ill-will but no more activity. Again, all was on the shoulders of a handful of people. Mr & Mrs Matheson, in Dennistoun, were the Party's longest serving stalwarts but had insufficient support to carry out anything approaching a campaign. Only three identifiable activists were known to me. Eoin Grant had been in London Branch, where, if past experience was any guide, distance from Scotland prompted some oddly unhelpful public statements and press comments. Eoin had been affected to some extent by this experience of exile, and had felt some temptation to follow where the NPS unwisely led. Fortunately, he was friendly with the Smarts, and his genuine patriotism and kindly temperament made him a good colleague as the years passed. We found that we shared an interest in the repertoire of political songs, many as printed in the Rebels' Ceilidh Song Book produced mainly by Bill Kellock and his pals in Bo'ness. On post-Conference, post-Council, post by-election occasions, whenever our paths crossed, Eoin would demand that we reprise our duet of the "John McLean March" by Hamish Henderson. It was a happy ritual, and I was grateful for the reliable warmth of his companionship. He went back and forth to London during his working life but in death he came home, and I joined John Innes, Neil MacCallum, and Peter Wright and others to scatter his ashes on the field of Bannockburn.

Eoin's usual companion was Hugh Watson, whom I did not know so well, but was a shrewd and hard-working member in a difficult time and area. They were joined by George Hamilton, who had long experience in Trade Union activity, which made him a very useful adviser for an organisation sadly lacking in people with such experience. George had found himself on the opposite side of past negotiations from Tom Gibson and these two, while forgiving to some extent, were not thinking of forgetting. However, this little group kept the SNP a presence in the East.

Apart from these early and immediate demands on me I began a steady and predictable schedule of Party work. I visited some branch or C.A. usually twice a week. Sometimes the visit was an intense pep-talk for members, but more often it was extended to a public meeting, whose purpose was to spread our arguments and seek to make converts and attract them into membership. Several branches had made efforts to expand into nearby areas, and I went to hold meetings intended for interested local people to come and give us a hearing.

In some places our work was suggested and assisted by individuals anxious to help. It has always been apparent to anyone who gives the matter any thought that SNP advances have been sparked off by some local well-regarded person. This fact confirmed me in my view that the Party ought, at the earliest possible stage, to establish in people's minds the fact that it was wholly ordinary and normal. Those outside had been conditioned into assuming that the Party was daft, eccentric, obsessive, lawless, and may be dangerous. It might attract good humoured laughter from those who found it funny, but those who found it funny all too often moved on to finding it ridiculous. No handicap, no greater obstacle to progress than that kind of feeling, stood in the way of any advance we could hope for.

For this reason I did everything I could to counter the image which the public had too often been given of posturing and display, however well-intentioned. I sought less drama and more organisation.

It was Murdo Young who suggested that we should plan to expand using our existing areas of comparative strength, Perth and Stirling. For this reason we attempted to start a branch in Crieff. The meeting came at the end of a bus journey – my only means of transport – from Glasgow, and I arrived, as always, needing time to recover from travel sickness. Only the Hall janitor and the local sponsor were present, so the enlightenment of Crieff had to wait for a year or two.

We had plans for West Stirling, and for the first time found that we had a volunteer ready to act on his own initiative. One Sunday afternoon I was visited in Glasgow by two young men on a motorbike, recently entered into civilian life from service in the RAF. The visitor, seeking help in starting a branch, was Ian Macdonald, who thus entered upon the first of his many services to the SNP. He was hoping to start a branch in Balfron, and, at his invitation, David Rollo and I went along to his meeting. His plan worked, and the branch gradually took strength and shape.

By coincidence a connection with Ian's later personal life occurred when I went with Murdo to a public meeting in Clackmannan. In the audience, and remaining to discuss the possible future branch, were Douglas Drysdale, and members of his family. So these two meetings secured for the Party its future National Organiser and a future Vice-Chairman and Executive Vice-Chairman.

Moving further afield, John Gilchrist, from Guildtown, had a brother in Dumfries, and he might be ready to try to form a branch. To encourage him we arranged to hold our next year's National Conference in Dumfries and held public meetings in preparation. Having ventured so far south we tried to repeat the attempt, and David Rollo, on an evening of thick fog, drove us to Annan, where we arrived as the organiser had given us up for lost. The last attempt for the time being was in Kilmarnock, where we had found one or two young supporters willing to try to build a branch there.

Back at the centre of things, we organised what was a new venture, a training weekend. We rented from the Boys' Brigade their Carronvale Training Centre at Larbert, and there we had seminars and discussions from people as expert as we could attract. The event was a great success, even though conditions appropriate for the Boys' Brigade were rather testing for middle-aged participants. Greatly to their credit members who were of an age well past the date when sleeping in bunk-beds in dormitories was their normal habit, all entered into the spirit of the event, which proved a very helpful bonding exercise as well as a political seminar. The social highlight which sticks in my mind was George Dott at the piano, singing "McGinty's Meal and Ale" with gusto.

Constituency work went on in spite of these Party-serving activities. Bob Porteous had devised a clever way of canvassing without appearing to do so. He organised a series of what he termed "political teas". Invitations to tea in the Lea Park Hotel, Grangemouth, were put through local doors welcoming all who cared to come along. There were no costs to those who came, their invitations served as their tickets. We had a modest meal of sandwiches, sausage rolls and the like, and then I would give the political message relevant to the moment. Entertainment was provided on either side of my address, by artistes like Bobby Christie, a very gifted and popular fiddler, and William Mundie, a bass singer from whose repertoire I learned songs not previously heard, all encouraging patriotic enthusiasm. Sometimes there was a supporting speaker, and at the end Bob would thank all who had accepted our invitations and hoped they had enjoyed their evening. On the way out, sly little plates had been left as a silent expression of hope for a donation. Bob believed, correctly I am sure, that we raised more money than selling tickets would have done. He tried to suggest his scheme to other constituencies, but I don't recall hearing of any imitations.

Some specific jobs fell to me on behalf of the Party. John Lindsay, a BBC producer in Scotland, managed to secure approval for a TV broadcast featuring Nationalists. He had been advised, by whom I never learned, that Nationalists brought together would fight, so he adopted a remarkable scheme. He invited four speakers, but had them attend on different occasions. Each was filmed speaking on points made off-camera by the director of the programme and his aides, and then the four separate contributions were editorially

61

faked up to make audiences think we had been on a kind of panel, of the sort now familiar in "Question Time".

The four contributors were chosen to represent what the outside world saw as varying, but equally ranked factions of the Nationalist movement. It was J.M. Reid who privately made the point to me that the SNP was only one Nationalist-sect among several. He was nowhere nearly ready to see that that the Convention was on the verge of dissolution, and that Congress was essentially a refuge for all who had feuded with the Party and had flounced out, or had never felt ready to submit themselves to any collective discipline. I argued then that the Party was in fact a kind of parent body, to which in the fullness of time all who wanted Home Rule would have to return. So indeed it has turned out, and in the past fifty years we have seen high office in the Party held by persons once active in these other bodies.

The actual filming was a triumph of improvisation over absurd inadequacy. The film camera was set on a kind of gallery at one end of the studio, and the contributor sat, posed and angled as if he was one of a semi-circle. When the crew came to set me up they found that I was sitting in a low chair which could not be raised, and I was short in stature and they could do nothing about that either. So they propped the chair up on piles of magazines, adding to each of the four piles until they got the height required.

The other participants, one had been and two were to follow on some other date, were J.M. Reid, Robert Blair Wilkie and Oliver Brown. I knew all three and would have fought with none, but perhaps better safe than sorry. The final oddity of the whole business was that I never saw the film, as I did not own a TV set until some four years afterwards, in 1962. Those who did see it seemed pleased enough.

The BBC at the time was of course denying the Party access to its channels, and we had been keeping up a barrage of complaint about this. For some reason our complaints must have touched a nerve, and we were invited to send a deputation to meet with BBC Scotland's Controller, Melville Dinwoodie. He was a man who I am sure would have believed all his life, in what was once a widely held and seriously argued opinion, that Scotland had no need of a Parliament because she already had the General Assembly of the Church of Scotland. Most people under the age of 80 will find it almost impossible to believe that perfectly ordinary people could hold a view so absurd.

We – David Rollo, Robert McIntyre and I – met Mr Dinwoodie whose annoyance with us he made no attempt to hide. After some talk back and forth, he offered what was, to him, the clinching argument. If we gave you access to broadcasting we would have to give it to the Communists. And why not? I asked him, and there the interview ended.

The campaign continued afterwards, David to plan and equip what later became Radio Free Scotland, and I represented the Party at a demonstration in Trafalgar Square which we shared with Plaid Cymru, the I.L.P. and Common Wealth. There I met for the first time Gwynfor Evans and J.E. Jones of the Plaid, and a lady from Common Wealth who had some remarkable tales of the Queen Mother and a nobleman whose title she could not properly pronounce. Every time I recall this event I remember the drama, not of the speeches, but of the symbolic music. We had a small music group who played the Welsh anthem, "Scots wha Ha'e" for us, the "Internationale" for the I.L.P. and "Jerusalem" for Common Wealth. In years to come Labour have pinched the tune as well as ideas from that now forgotten party.

Every so often someone has raised again the notion that if we wanted to counter the Tory and Labour giants we should form an alliance with the Liberals. It is tempting to assume that the Liberals are really just electioneers without much partisan commitment. That was not how things turned out. I was at two meetings attempting to form a pact with the Liberal Party. On the first occasion Robert led Frank Yeaman and myself to meet the then Liberal chairman in Scotland, Charles Johnston, and his Treasurer colleague, Mr McPake. On the second occasion we met with David Steel and Russell Johnstone. Mr Steel was pleasant, courteous and shifty. Mr Johnstone made it clear that he considered us detestable, which spoke well of his frankness and very badly of his common sense. He was one prominent person to see in Nationalism, even Scottish Nationalism, a potentially Fascist doctrine. The meeting while not breaking up in abuse got us nowhere.

Mischief making in the Party had very commonly been a feature of people calling themselves "a ginger group". The phrase tends to attract the attention of journalists and gives a semblance of righteous purpose to persons temperamentally disgruntled with leadership imperfections. Given that the Party had enjoyed no chance or sign of success since 1945, impatience had to be expected, and a lack of ginger on the part of the Party's officials was detected by many members from time to time. This feeling had helped to encourage some supporters of the NPS, and prompted members to look around for possible activity. It was a new member who came up with the answer.

There appeared in Glasgow, working for the Daily Express, an editorial journalist, Ian Howard. Identifying himself as a supporter wishing to help, he put forward a proposal that a fund-raising group might be set up, each member pledging to pay a small sum each week, and receipt cards would be provided. Ian offered himself as organiser, and he took up his post with a table and chair in the hall of the Elmbank Street offices.

The venture seemed to be working well enough for it to continue, and it was the subject of official record at National Council where Ian explained and reported upon the project thus far. At how early a stage he tied his plan to an opinion that the rest of us were sloths and failures I don't know. He may have formed that opinion before coming forward with his plan, or he may have been disappointed by our failure to support and provide for the next step. Anyhow, by way of gingering us up, Ian sold the Glasgow organisation on the idea of a massive entry into municipal elections.

With admirable vigour and persuasiveness he coaxed us into selecting candidates, planning where to stand and seeking financial backing. With his journalistic skills and contacts he arranged for the publishing of an election address, with contents covering the whole city, and a column for a message from each candidate.

Glasgow municipal elections had always seemed to me a distressing combination of class-war, sectarian conflict and financial corruption, and I had no thought of participation. However, it was put to me that it was my duty as Party Chairman to give a lead in this campaign, and thus it came about that I was selected to contest Shettleston. Once selected, and contrary to advance promises, I was left very much on my own to cover the doors and acres of Lightburn. On one day which sticks in the mind, I had two helpers, my wife and a friend of ours from GUSNA's days. This young lady had to go on later to some social engagement for which she required to carry a pink umbrella and a pink hat-box. She gallantly climbed up and down stairs and closes, but gradually showed such signs of fatigue that mere chivalry required that I should carry her burden. It was a fine sunny afternoon, and the streets were quiet and empty which was just as well. A male candidate seen canvassing while in possession of pink finery would not have been well regarded.

The campaign ended inevitably in crushing defeat. Shettleston had been seen as the likeliest source of support; and indeed it produced our best result. For that I was indebted to David Cathcart and his Uddingston colleagues a few miles along the road, in particular an Uddingston member, John McGough who was my agent.

I don't know if Ian was just disappointed, or if his pressure to fight the campaign was seen as some sort of test which I and the Party had now failed. For whatever reason he now became very troublesome. He was to be found in close co-operation with Angus and Bobby, and had been associated with them in the attempted use of Miss McCloskey to make trouble.

His skills in publicity and propaganda were very real, but his tabloid-trained background tempted him into mistakes. For instance, Glasgow's papers were given photographs of Ian's house, disfigured by a painted message which read "Home Rule Howard; Scottish Scum." Since he was not likely to have become widely identified as a Nationalist Captain by our opponents, the general assumption was that he had written it himself as a talking point in campaigning.

Meanwhile David Rollo's work had produced Radio Free Scotland, and Gordon Wilson had joined him in organising transmissions. Just as had happened when the Stone of Destiny was taken, anyone of Nationalist opinions was trying desperately hard to look guilty, so now involvement in the secret Radio was something to brag about. I was never called upon to play any part in RFS. The nearest I came to participation was when Murdoch Young and I transported radio equipment in two great heavy boxes which we stowed below the stairs in an Alexander's double deck bus. When we reached our destination at Larbert Cross, where it was planned to transmit from the home of Russell Hill's mother, Murdo and I had a struggle with the boxes and was grateful for the help of a kind police constable standing on the dismounting platform. An article appeared in "Illustrated" magazine, purporting to show a broadcast being organised, with photographs including one of a robust kilted person climbing a ladder. He was pretty clearly identifiable as a fierce NPS partisan, so the origins of the fake story were fairly obvious. It did seem, however, that some journalistic influence and expertise was involved and after a long period of tactful silence, John Smart who had had enough of Ian's scheming openly identified him at National Council as being responsible for the "Illustrated" article which, of course, was invention.

Relations now had drifted into hostility, Ian's contempt for the Party's lack of drive being countered by an official distaste for his dishonest versions of events. At this point a by-election was called in Kelvingrove. As before we had to argue the pros and cons of contesting, and since we had neither the local organisation nor the funds which the Constitution said we must have before undertaking a contest, the NEC decided that the Party would not contest.

Such a decision would readily be seen as failure by our critics, and the NEC ruling was defied by a few members who publicly announced their support for a candidate, officially independent but going to accept the Liberal whip. This candidate, David Murray was a Home Rule supporter without a doubt but his acceptance of a Liberal label made him the candidate of a rival party in our eyes. Any Party member publicly supporting the campaign of such a candidate was in breach of the rules, as well as showing defiance of the wishes and decision of the appropriate Party authority. For their persevering insistence on challenging the NEC, Ian Howard, Angus McIntosh and Bobby Stevenson were reported to National Council with a motion that they be expelled. I was personally entirely certain that this had to be done, because the deep-rooted hostility to the Party's elected committee was all too obvious. I pointed out to the culprits that I had to move their expulsion because not to do so would tend to justify their opinion that I was a cowardly incompetent.

As always on such occasions many delegates were inclined to find excuses for the members under censure. But the motion was passed. Ian had a final shot at the NEC when we, in desperate financial straits as usual, rented a room in Elmbank Street to a commercial firm. This he described as "taking English gold" in a bid to turn the members against us.

As time passed, Angus and Bobby came back into the fold, and were good and admirable workers for the Party. They found it easier it seemed, if I wasn't there.

Ian, I only saw once after these events. He arrived in a press car to attend John MacCormick's funeral at Bedlay Cemetery. Always perfectly good-humoured aside from the argument of the moment, he introduced me to his driver as the man who expelled him from the SNP. When I suggested that he had pretty loudly sought martyrdom he just grinned and made no further argument.

To do their little bit to expose the failure of the SNP to take useful initiatives, Scottish National Congress decided to appeal publicly for the support of the Soviet Union. Just why the goodwill of that particular power was thought to make Scotland's cause more attractive only the Congress strategists could ever understand. For most people the wartime popularity of the Red Army had been destroyed by the cynical occupation of Czechoslovakia and the attack on Hungary in 1956. Any courtship of Soviet goodwill would be sufficiently damaging for the Party as to require us to disclaim the attempt and define Congress as yet another body which no SNP member could join and remain one of our members.

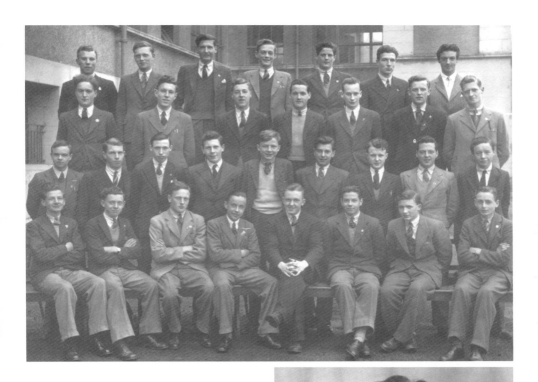

Top: Greenock High School,
Fifth Year, 1943. James Halliday,
third from right front row.
(Photo: Prophet)

Graduation from Glasgow University in
1952 with an Hons. Degree in History.
(Photo: Annan)

James Halliday married Olive Campbell in Glasgow on 12 July 1952.
(Photo: Scottish Press Agency Ltd.),

PARLIAMENTARY ELECTION, 1955

To the Electors of

STIRLING, FALKIRK AND GRANGEMOUTH BURGHS

JAMES HALLIDAY

JAMES HALLIDAY was brought up in the Scottish democratic tradition, to regard all men as brothers and to respect the views of others. He is a teacher of history in Lanarkshire, and can claim a knowledge of social problems in widely varied areas. He is able also to look at Scotland against a European background, and as a historian has an understanding of the origins of many present-day problems.

James Halliday and Alex Meikle keep an eye on election volunteers in 1955.
(Photo: F Johnston & Co Ltd)

All those who attended the SNP Conference 1956 at the Allan Water Hotel, Bridge of Allan.
Front Row: George Leask, Bruce Watson, Arthur Donaldson, Tom Gibson, Fiona Smart, Helen McIntosh, Olive Bruce, Vi Donaldson.
Second Row: Murdoch Young, Ian Howard, Olive Halliday, Robert MacIntyre, Angus MacIntosh, David Rollo.
Third Row: Willie Gillespie, Russell Hill, James Halliday, John Frew, Andy Bruce (London), John Smart, Bobby Stevenson, unknown.
Fourth Row: Mr Nicholson, unknown, Mr McIntosh, unknown, Ian Smith, Eoin Grant, Hugh Watson.
Back Row: Robin Leask, John Gilchrist, unknown, Mrs Joanne Watson, unknown.
Known Absentees: Robert Porteous (Grangemouth), James Ellis, Robert Campbell (Stirling), Bruce Cockie (Aberdeen), Robert Tennant, Malcolm Shaw (Perth), Frank Yeaman (Edinburgh), Alex Aitken (Edinburgh), Norrie Douglas (Hamilton), David Cathcart (Uddingston), Wm S Orr (Dumbarton).
(Photo: D Ross Robertson)

'A Political Tea' Lea Park, Grangemouth, c. 1958. James Halliday third from the right back row. Phyllis McCloskey, middle of front row.

James Halliday's adoption meeting to stand in West Fife in 1970. L to R: James Lees, Pat Lochtie, Jim Thomson, Winifred Ewing, Peter Wright, James Halliday, Bob Patrick, Ray Bald, Alan Robertson, James Thomson. *(Photo: Peter Leslie)*

SNP St Ninian's branch Burns Supper in Stirling in the mid '70s.
L to R: Roger Mullin, Robert Campbell, Margaret Ewing and James Halliday.

James Halliday and Billy Wolfe walk down the Royal Mile to Holyrood for the opening of the Scottish Parliament. 9 October 2004. *(Photo: Gordon Wright)*

The Scots Independent team in Tillicoultry, June 2006. Back Row: Tom Preston, Kenneth Fee, Margery Fee. Middle Row: David Rollo, Olive Halliday, Lillian Macdonald, Denholm Christie. Front Row: Helen Davidson, Norma Preston, James Halliday, Jim Lynch, Myra Christie. *(Photo: Joan McCann)*.

SNP MSPs newly elected to the Scottish Parliament. 7 May 2011. *(Photo: Gordon Wright)*

CHAPTER 5

1958 – 60 Last Election in Stirling

In 1958 I moved from Glasgow to Dunfermline, and there began to work in wholly unfamiliar circles. There was no branch, but some identifiable supporters and before long a branch was functioning, never strong, but capable of carrying forward the Party's work in the town.

We were eventually ready to hold a full blown public meeting in the Co-operative Halls in Randolph Street. In speaking that night I argued that the Conservatives would never win in that constituency. They were always preaching that a Nationalist vote was wasted, whereas the truly wasted vote was that given to a party so widely disliked and so socially unacceptable as to be un-electable. We had at least the potential to defeat Labour if voters really wished to do that, as we did not carry the kind of baggage which crippled the Tories.

Arithmetically, I was perfectly correct, though I knew the argument wouldn't be widely accepted. What came as a surprise was the fury of Douglas Tulloch, the editor of the Dunfermline Press. I had always assumed that local editors need not be much impressed by the sort of debating tactics that political speakers might use, but to find such outrage was unlooked for. He was the Session Clerk of the church which I attended and it was a sobering discovery for me to know that he was so hostile to my politics. It was quite a landmark, because it showed me that most people were entirely uninterested, and was perfectly affable and smiling until they felt a surge of anger when they felt we might be making some impact.

The same sort of discovery came with the General Election of 1959. We had five candidates instead of two. Robert and I repeated our campaigns of 1955, and were joined by Arthur Donaldson in Kinross and West Perth, Sandy Milne in Aberdeen South and David Rollo in Hamilton. The numbers were better, but the campaign was disappointing.

Goodwill was less apparent. The local press were less civil and we ended up only 100 votes better off. In Perth our strength was much as before, and in the other three to have contested at all was progress. One benefit was the arrival among us of supporters who had come into the branches in these four years. Robert McIntyre had taken advantage of his release from the Chair to enter local politics in Stirling. He now led a strong group which included Robert Campbell, and had recruited several very effective councillors. In particular I now came to know and value Helen Davidson. Helen's range of interests, abilities and experience gave me the greatest possible help in all subsequent years, in particular arranging broadcasting opportunities and above all as Secretary and true organiser of the Election Committee in its training, selection and administration. For myself and many others in the Party she came to be relied upon as the wisest and most trustworthy of colleagues.

In the run up to the election I had been deputed by the NEC to make our Party's election broadcast, which I duly did. The young ladies of my Higher class in Dunfermline sent me a goodwill message for the campaign and promised "to listen attentively and disagree entirely." Some were sadly truthful but others as it turned out were so sympathetic to our message as to alarm their parents.

The move to Dunfermline had opened up new areas of possible expansion. Murdo and I drove, he having acquired a car by this time, to Buckhaven to see if we could follow up visits to Kirkcaldy which had uncovered some interest but not yet a branch. In Buckhaven we met with enough support to leave a steering committee to carry matters forward. One of those most clearly ready to commit himself was a young man from the North East who had come to a local government post in Fife. This was Peter Wright with whom I was to enjoy friendship and Party work for what is now close on 50 years.

Our election campaign in 1959 was little more than a revival of 1955. We had perhaps a few more people to work but still came nowhere near having the numbers to do a proper canvass, and we had a support as scattered as it could be, so any hope of effective "knocking" on election day was faint.

The general feeling was much less friendly, and though disappointed, I was not surprised by our failure to make real progress. My disappointment was shared by the activists. Bob and Murdo were not visibly downhearted, and Stirling branch had worked well enough to keep them with fight still in them.

For my part, I knew that my personal life would now work against my remaining as candidate. My work in Dunfermline was rewarding, interesting, but more demanding and I would not find working for the Party and for the constituency possible. In any case, both constituency and Party might well be thinking of a change. My thoughts of ending my days as candidate were encouraged by the reaction of the Stirling councillor, who perhaps had not yet begun to think about the prospects for the Party, and contented himself with the anxious question, "I wonder how this will affect my seat?"
There was one interesting follow-up to the 1959 campaign. Soon after it was ended I was told by Donald Cameron that Malcolm MacPherson had asked him to arrange a meeting with me "for a talk". Donald sounded very intrigued. I thought merely that Mr MacPherson was just extending the courteous behaviour of the campaign into private life.

We met in the Temperance Café in Falkirk – a favourite haunt of the MP. We talked of the campaign, the likely course of events under the new MacMillan government and then I found myself being questioned about my own political intentions and ambitions. Did I mean to go on contesting elections in an apparently hopeless cause? Had I never thought that I might more sensibly enter the mainstream of politics, and perhaps win an election? If I ever felt interested he would see that I met people who could help.

I didn't fully appreciate that I was being recruited, with the implications of backing from him to give me safe passage to the Labour Party and eventual nomination. Incredible as it may seem I had no wish to become a professional, even an MP, and I certainly had no thought of actively taking part in politics for any purpose other than securing independence. In a fairly light –hearted way, I batted aside the seriousness of his inquiries, and we parted civilly but with nothing in the way of a result.

71

It was Donald Cameron who upbraided me on the grounds that I could have worked for Home Rule as a Labour candidate with a greater likelihood of being elected and therefore having a chance to do anything.

I remembered this meeting when not long afterwards a Plaid Cymru young rising star, close disciple of Gwynfor Evans, went over to Labour. In a glorious irony Gwynfor was soon afterwards elected as MP for Carmarthen. His deserting protégé became Elystan Morgan MP (Labour). Gwynfor never offered any public reproach, but to lose a friend and colleague, tempted by ambition, was a sad disappointment.

I mentioned all this to Robert McIntyre, and learned that he too had been propositioned about securing his career in the Labour Party. I imagine others have had the same experience.

I told the NEC that I would leave the Chair. Dunfermline was not such a central point in relation to the Party as a whole as Glasgow was. I chaired my last Conference in Stirling's Albert Hall, telling the delegates that I felt it was time for a change, and I was going before too many of them agreed with me.

Through those years, the branch which earned my greatest gratitude and admiration was not any of my own constituency three, excellent though they were. The branch which extended the greatest courtesy to their Chairman was Dumbarton. They met me off train or bus, had everything well organised, and saw me safely back to bus stop or station. In many other places heads might scarcely turn to say "Goodnight"!

On leaving the Chair I had been elected to the newly-created post of Vice-President, so I was still involved in election planning. At the National Council following my retiral, I was hailed by Dan McDonald from West Lothian, looking very much like a man with good news to offer. He told me, though no formal announcement had yet been made, that West Lothian had found themselves a candidate for a by-election, a local man with good community ties, to the industry of the area through family tradition, to the youth, through the Scout Movement, and to cultural groups through the Saltire Society. His name he said, and told me to expect an announcement soon, was William Wolfe.

Oddly enough I knew of the family firm, through a visit with a farm equipment supplier, Bob Begg from Tarbolton. I had travelled with him to the forge at Bathgate, though I cannot claim to have met Billy quite so early.

I did not cite West Lothian in my list of identifiably active branches. That is because in my time in office, it was semi-detached. It did its own thing. It was not open to pressure or liable to discipline because it mattered not at all whether the Party approved or not. No permission was thought at all relevant and no sanction was feared. What was known was the happy, joyous, commanding group centring mainly on Bo'ness. They knew how to co-operate and they knew how to have an impact on their own community. We knew something of the exploits of Bill Kellock through his brother in Perthshire, and through the excellent Rebels' Ceilidh Song Book which was a cultural icon for the SNP at the time.

Some individual members had emerged into the wider Scottish world from time to time, usually Rob Kerr, who came to National Council sometimes, and Angus McGillveray. When shortly West Lothian's intention to contest was made known and the name of their candidate was announced, all of us with an interest in election preparation were greatly heartened. We did not have any inside knowledge about their thinking, but we knew that they were capable of great enthusiasm and vigour. Arthur was quick to establish contacts and things moved rapidly forward.

For the reliable story of subsequent events we are now fortunate to have Gordon Wilson's history of the Party, "The Turbulent Years: 1960-1990". His narrative begins with the start of Arthur Donaldson's years as Chairman. It was our great good fortune that Arthur in retirement was free to do the rounds of the Party with greater ease and freedom than I had ever been able to do. It is my one major regret that I was never in a position to carry out proper evangelising work throughout the country, as Arthur did so very effectively. I have been intrigued to have realised that everywhere Arthur Donaldson worked on our behalf, the time came that the Party held every seat in those areas. Moray, Angus, West Perthshire, Tayside all were part of Arthur's vineyard, and, in a period, when he extended his range, he provided the basis for later victory in Galloway.

I now became much less active. I did continue to attend to various party requirements, but not now with the same degree of obligation. So I missed much of the work in what proved an exciting decade. The most important fact was that we had a series of by-elections, which we were able to use to gain publicity, train ourselves and improve our organisational efficiency. For this last fact we were indebted to Ian Macdonald who had become National Organiser. The idea of the appointment arose from Ian's own feelings of urgency, and from Robert McIntyre's wisdom in working out how a Party about as wealthy as a church mouse could possibly maintain an official of such importance. I couldn't understand how it was done, but these two worked it out somehow, and we immediately made ourselves more effective.

We had a constitutional requirement, imposed because of many memories of doing ourselves down when attempting tasks beyond our powers. We would not contest unless we had in the constituency concerned, members on the ground and money to fight the campaign. For this reason we had refrained from contesting several by-elections, Kelvingrove being one, and the time had come that press and public really had begun to assume that we would play no part perhaps ever again.

This provides me with the one significant action that I can claim in the early 60s. When a by-election was called in Bridgeton where we had neither members nor money, the immediate assumption was that we would once again stand aside. It had become clear to me that our people were very close to writing us off altogether, and I therefore spoke and moved in favour of contesting, constitution or not, because if we did not we might as well shut up shop and go home.

So we contested, and Ian MacDonald fought a campaign of quite improbable vigour and determination which was rewarded with almost a fifth of the votes cast. It amazed me, because it showed that there was in Glasgow an unsuspected pool of support.

Gordon has provided the most convenient and informative summary about the other by-elections which followed, West Lothian (June 1962), Glasgow Woodside (November 1962), Kinross and West Perthshire (October 1963), Dundee West (November 1963) and Dumfries (December 1963).

I spoke for Arthur in Kinross and Crieff, but played no part elsewhere. Arthur's prospects were already adversely affected by the fact that the newly selected British Prime Minister was the Tory candidate. There was another underhand piece of mischief to which Gordon does not refer. In Dundee West Dr James Lees was going to be our candidate in a constituency where no very great hopes of victory existed. On the other hand, Arthur had done well in West Perth in 1959, and we felt had very right to hope for a good result.

We had forgotten the capacity of the Liberal Party for trickery. Contesting Dundee had never crossed their minds, but they now had the gall to suggest that we should stand down and allow them a free hand in West Perth, and in return they would stand down and graciously allow us to have West Dundee unmolested. The Liberals were not then so familiar to us as they have since become, and their sneaky arrogance in seeing themselves for no good reason as a "major" party, far beyond ours in importance, is deeply annoying. Even worse is the readiness of press and public to talk up and write up the Liberals as if they represented anything coherent at all beyond providing a temporary escape value for pent up irritability in the voters at election time.

Another of their distinguishing marks was then, and since, the desire to use elections to push into the public gaze someone whom they held in great esteem for their own reasons. Liberals in Orkney and Shetland were really just for maintaining Jo Grimond in his public position. Maitland Mackie was spoken of with awe among Liberals in the North

East, and in West Perth their obedient devotion was bestowed upon Duncan Millar of Remony. These three gentlemen were good and intelligent people, but their power in the eyes of Liberal supporters made it look as though Scotland was making it possible for politics to become again the sport of the bunnet lairds just as in past times.

Their intrigue didn't bring them much joy. They did not elect Mr Duncan Millar but they did cut savagely into the vote which Arthur Donaldson might justly have expected.

Billy Wolfe's vote in West Lothian gave the Party a great boost to confidence and morale, and he and his West Lothian supporters became from that moment onwards a major element in the Party's growth.

As 1964 approached, the Party had to intensify preparations for the General Election which would be required in that year. My virtual holiday from campaigning was interrupted at this stage by a visit from James Lees who had been building up the Party's presence in Kirkcaldy and had been keeping a benevolent eye on Fife. He asked me to return to activity, appealing to my loyalty, and offering some flattery in case loyalty proved ineffective.

His proposal was that I should stand for the Party in Dunfermline. He paid a further visit accompanied by James Cook who had been invigorating the Party in Inverkeithing. I would rather have stood in Dunfermline than anywhere else in the country. I was happy, settled, successful in professional terms, and with good and developing contacts in the town. But I had to refuse. I felt that it would be improper to be campaigning among people whose children I was teaching. I was, I think, over sensitive and over scrupulous, but that was the decision.

Regrets about Dunfermline are enhanced by reading Gordon's account of the revival of 1964 onwards, in which I played no real part beyond speaking at some election meetings in 1964 and 1966. As a result of this inactivity I had no prior understanding of the plans for George Leslie's candidacy in Pollok. In fact my interest in Pollok had been prompted by the Tory experience there, rather than ours. An old university associate, Robert Kernohan, had been defeated thanks to the construction of Labour-sheltering new housing estates in the constituency. His successor, now Tory candidate, was Esmond Wright, who had taught both Bob and myself, and was a man of outstanding charisma, whose Tory politics came as a great surprise and disappointment to his friends; Esmond was hardly a run-of-the-mill candidate, and his presence forced the Tory campaign on to a rather higher plane than was usual in Glasgow.

George's vote was encouraging, as Billy's had been, and things were becoming more lively altogether. About now I was being told by Phyllis McCloskey of her experiences in a Scots Law class in the Commercial College, being taken by a Mrs Ewing. She sang the praises of Mrs Ewing, for whom she predicted a great political career if she chose to seek it. As time passed I realised that Mrs Ewing was one and the same with Winnie Woodburn of 20 years ago. I was intrigued to know that Winnie was now showing her interest, and when Robert told me that Miss McCloskey had urged him to speak to Mrs Ewing, I gave him the most vigorous encouragement to do just that. Finding candidates was always a challenge which Robert enjoyed, and so it came about that on a winter evening in Glasgow, at a presentation dinner in honour of Tom Gibson, I met Winnie and Stewart, and heard of the up-coming nomination and campaign in Hamilton. David Rollo had blazed the trail in Hamilton, and the nucleus of the Party's organisation in Hamilton I knew from the mid '50s. Norrie Douglas in particular had been a steady and constant presence, and I expected that we might do quite well, perhaps as well as in Pollok, though not perhaps as well as in West Lothian. As we talked, Winnie was looking at me in puzzlement, and then said, "But Jimmy, I'm going to win." I tried feebly to suggest that victory was not the result of an act of will. We all <u>wanted</u> to win, but it was not in our power to dictate the outcome. Winnie remained unconvinced and clearly continued to presume that Fate would respond to her instructions.

When the by-election was held, I found myself on the eve-of-poll speaking for Winnie in Larkhall, where my fellow speaker was the famous and popular Ludovic Kennedy. I felt rather superfluous in such company, and I turned to talk to some of Winnie's local supporters. There too I found that I had a lot to learn about my role in the evening. I was taken under the wing of a remarkably vivacious and attractive young woman, blonde, in a scarlet blazer and white skirt. I have been lucky enough to find that a sense of the ridiculous has saved me from showing admiration too openly, but though I smiled inwardly as this girl explained politics to me I did not find her in the least ridiculous. Surprising perhaps, but she seemed to know what she was talking about. Such was my first meeting with Margo MacDonald. I saw in her that night a political talent of the greatest promise, but of course, so did everyone else.

Winnie continued to predict victory. Arthur had concluded that she might well be right. On election night a little quartet of ex-GUSNA members watched on television, Jarvis and I, Olive and Isobel, and the years fairly rolled away as we rose rejoicing to see Winnie's victory. Any set-backs after that night were temporary. There would be no return to the bystander status of all the Party's previous years. Even when Winnie lost at the General Election, just as Robert had done in 1945, Donald Stewart kept us in the arena in 1970 and Margo joined him in 1973, and 1974 elections were just round the corner. If ever one key unlocked vital doors, Winnie's victory in Hamilton was the key to all the Party's later flourishing.

CHAPTER 6

DUNDEE

In 1967, on the night Celtic won the European Cup, James Lees and I were in Dundee, sent by the NEC to investigate a dispute among Party members in that city.

I had twice set foot in Dundee, once to visit a friend who from time to time worked there, and once in response to an advert for a History teacher. It seemed that the advert was published only to allow the Depute Director of Education to see what a graduate in History and nothing else looked like. He wondered why I hadn't done Maths. I confessed that I didn't come close to understanding Algebra. He looked with sad pity, and paid my rail fare, and that was that.

Now we were meeting our own people and listened while they explained what their dispute was about. It was unfortunately not at all made clear, and Dr Lees and I were left to reach some conclusions on the impressions we had formed of the people in the argument, rather than upon a real understanding of the argument itself.

I had met Tom McFettridge when Malcolm Shaw introduced him to me at his first National Council meeting some years before. Tom had a brisk manner, fluent and articulate and was an expert at spotting someone up to what he always called "the capers". As the meeting progressed he was supported by evidence from several colleagues, in particular David White and Rose Webster. David sometimes let his own certainty make him forget that his hearers needed to be told more than they knew thus far, but he came across to Dr Lees and myself as one telling a true story. Rose was quiet but very unshaken in her evidence and again we felt we could believe her explanation.

This meeting was of Camperdown Branch, and the rival faction which we were yet to investigate was Downfield Branch. No Dundee member at the meeting took issue with the version of events given by the branch officials, McFettridge, White and Miss

Webster. Any contradiction or hostility was offered by the Party's Convenor of the Organisation Committee, Russell Thomson. His report then and at subsequent NEC meetings was packed with details running into one another and spilling in a torrent on the bewildered listeners' ears, with the name "Miss Webster" ringing out regularly and frequently as he gave his version.

From several persons we heard mention of one George McLean. In Dundee they pronounce that name, for some reason, in the English fashion as though it was "McLeen". I had only quite recently come to understand the point of the toothpaste advert and Dundee's pronunciation fixed the sales purpose in my mind.

McLean, it seemed, was in disagreement, on a wide range of issues, with the Camperdown members. Having heard the Camperdown story we, Robert Campbell and I, had to meet with McLean and branch in Downfield. When the NEC was eventually given our report, and Russell Thomson was able to suggest alternatives, decision and action was evaded and postponed. As might be expected, NEC members hoped that such disagreements would not happen at all, but if they did, avoiding as long as possible giving a ruling was the preferred course. In any case they couldn't be bothered working out the difference between Camperdown and Downfield, whose names they found terribly comical. For the first time in my experience I was tempted to understand, and see some merit in, the sour hostility of Grampian towards the Clyde valley. The bemused, confused and markedly lazy NEC pooh-poohed, and tush-tushed, and come-comed, and next-businessed and wondered why there was no branch called "Camperfield" and guffawed, until a really serious row broke out.

What the NEC did not appreciate, was that the Dundee internal clash was part of a wider crisis which developed from a conspiracy – again! – justifying itself by purporting to be a "ginger group". This one was smart enough to seize upon Scottish history and call itself the "1320 Group", encouraging everyone to bear in mind the Declaration of Arbroath and its place in the struggle for independence.

The 1320 Club is a study worth undertaking, particularly since wider histories of the Party give it little attention. In general it was very much an up-dated 55 Group and NPS, but with more suavity and literary quality. They even produced a quality magazine, "Catalyst", whose financing still prompts puzzled envy in me. Its activities had, as their goal, the capturing of branch office posts by the Group's sympathisers, so that in due course, the delegates from all these branches might be able to bring the entire Party under their control.

They seemed to enjoy the sympathy of the Convener of the Party's Organisation Committee, which added to the difficulty in agreeing how to deal with them. Some survivors of the NPS could be spotted from time to time in press reports - the press were of course overjoyed by the Party's latest embarrassment - and in the columns of the "Catalyst". The Group, however, had produced a leadership of its own, and they gave to it an even more disturbing profile.

The frankest comments on this topic are made by John Herdman in his booklet, "Poets, Pubs, Polls & Pillar Boxes" (Akros: Kirkcaldy 1999). As a younger man, in association with the persons he describes, his gradual awareness of the Group's blemishes is reassuring. Irreconcilable, awkward-squad, ex-SNP members are prominent. Our 1955 adversary, James Glendinning is there too. But most sinister, and enough in his own right to render his involvement undesirable, was Major Boothby, a man whose essential nastiness was to become abundantly and publicly clear in the years ahead.

I suppose that Russell Thomson was the 1320 field officer who recruited George McLean
I suppose that some was the 1320 field officer identified and recruited George McLean
and set him to take over Dundee.

McLean proved a very active associate, and under his leadership from his Downfield base, his chosen lieutenants formed purported branches in various Dundee wards.

By the time this was happening I had come to work in Dundee, so saw the rest of the story at close quarters. I attended meetings of the alleged branch nearest to home and found four or five people, not the slightest semblance of procedure, no minutes, no reports. We didn't even sit down, but strolled around chatting as the mood took the chairman. As had happened at other times in other cities, the organisation's basis was fraud. A man was chairman of one branch, secretary of another, perhaps treasurer of a third, and so on, branch office-bearers permutating themselves as best suited their purposes.

All this time pleas and warnings were coming from Tom McFettridge and David White who had seen McLean's work from its inception. Even the Chairman and the National Organiser were begged for intervention, but only soothing words were offered, as Tom told me as his frustration grew.

Belatedly I was dispatched to make one last attempt to stop the disruption. I met with some Downfield members, and told them about the wider picture, and how their branch had been involved in schemes of which they knew nothing. I told them of 1955, and of the similarities in the situation which we now faced. I told them of the 1320 Club constitution which said that members were not allowed to know who were the other members. It always amused me that the next clause explained how an EGM could be called by a member supported by enough signatures. How he would get them when he didn't know who to ask was nowhere explained. Remembering 1955, and with features of Major Boothby in mind, I warned them that they were in the presence of a Fascist-type coup attempt.

I should have known better. The man in the street, or in the branch, doesn't give much thought to Fascism, and can't be bothered making himself better informed. However, word went from the meetings, and I received a letter from an ex 55 Group stalwart, now a lawyer in training, telling me that I had given grief and hurt and other misfortunes, to the 1320 persons against whom I had warned the Downfield members. I replied only to let him know that I would welcome the chance to put the 1320 Constitution and various statements from its spokesmen before any panel of Political Scientists, and invite their judgement as to the Fascist content. With pity and forgiveness in mind, I refrained from asking the senior partner of the firm, where he was employed, and whose notepaper he had used, if he, the senior partner, was aware of this action of his not-quite-colleague. I heard no more about it.

Now, at last, the Party had had enough, and the 1320 Club was defined as the kind of body with whose principles and conduct we did not wish to associate and Party members could not be Club members at the same time.

The usual cries of outraged innocence were heard from various points in the land, but in Dundee the consequences were more serious than elsewhere. Mr McLean, unwilling to see his leadership status end, decided to set up in political business on his own account. His zest for the battle led him to a Party public meeting in Newport to be addressed by Arthur Donaldson. When time for questions arrived Mr McLean with cheerful belligerence began to do his best to put Arthur on the defensive. Not that Arthur had much difficulty in dealing with his questions, but Mr McLean, who had brought friends and family with him, left the floor to a lady of his group. With the sort of civility which political speakers are always wise to practise, Arthur answered courteously, and ended his answer by giving the questioner the name which he thought was hers – "Mrs McLean". The lady then protested that she had been incorrectly identified, and Arthur apologised to her and to Mrs McLean. From his seat in the front row Mr McLean, enjoying the turn of events, cried out, "As long as you didn't call her Mrs Donaldson." At this, aware of the malicious intent, Arthur stepped down from the platform and cuffed McLean. Again, shock, horror, outrage and glee from Mr McLean. Unfortunately this time he had the law on his side. Arthur was in due course tried and fined for assault, and the episode undoubtedly prompted him to retire as Party Chairman.

Mr McLean was not finished with us yet. He now formed a party of his very own, which he called the Scottish Labour Party. With this vehicle he set off on an ego-trip which led him to contest the Dundee East by-election in March 1973. He secured enough votes to deny Gordon Wilson the victory which he almost certainly would then have won.

This narrative of the Dundee East dispute and its aftermath has moved the Dundee story too far forward in time. Returning to 1967, I found that our members had been enjoying needling the Dundee West MP Peter Doig. Mr Doig's constituency officials were the highest, ablest top brass of Labour in the city. They knew how to deal with provocation like challenges to debate and such tricks, and thus simply ignored the SNP. Mr Doig, however, was more indignant at the insubordination of such lesser parties, and, losing discretion, publicly accepted the challenge to debate. His managers, particularly the much-feared J.L. Stewart, tried to ignore his decision, but publicity had now gone too far.

The trouble was that the baiting of Peter Doig had been the idea of Tom McFettridge and his Camperdown allies. They had now got their showdown, but they had not decided upon their speaker.

In the event I was asked to take on this sudden high profile in the city of which I still knew very little. Tom told me many years later that his closest colleagues had expected that the Party's most recent by-election star, George Leslie, would be invited. As Tom explained they didn't know anything about me, but he, as National Council delegate, did, and he argued them into accepting me.

We had a meeting to agree rules of the match, with J.L. Stewart, who fenced with all the professionalism of the highly-experienced Labour mandarin. It amused me, because he could not see that it genuinely did not matter to me what the order of speaking was, and when he fixed that to the advantage of his man he took it for granted that he had outwitted the simpleton. We agreed that Peter would get the last word, and after some worried thought, a neutral chairman was found in Jerry Kerr, manager of Dundee United, a man well-regarded, but of no known political convictions.

I always used to seek to make candidates feel confident by reminding them that if they knew their subject and believed in their cause they could stand up to anybody. I like to think that that Sunday afternoon in the St David's Halls, I went some way to proving my point. Like many, perhaps all, of his party and generation, Mr Doig came to the platform

84

assuming that all Nationalists were Tories, daft, ignorant, pointless and just nuisances. His points tended to be built on these assumptions, and it was not too difficult to present something more serious to the audience.

Peter was very serious in deploring all I stood for, but was perfectly civil. His supporters, perhaps quicker to realise that Nationalism was beginning to sound not such an unspeakable evil, became quite restless, and made Jerry Kerr intervene to keep the discussion in order. One young man, recently graduated from Dundee University was now beginning a career in the city's library service, which in time led him to highest professional success. That day, despite his intelligence and academic ability, his political bigotry shone in every expression which crossed his features, and in every jump and leap of angry outrage which greeted my explanation of Nationalist reasoning. He too has many modern counterparts.

One such was a man I had met several times before coming to Dundee. It was a regular annual engagement prompted, I think, by David Rollo, junior, when a student at the then Queen's College in Dundee, that I should travel from Dunfermline to speak to the Dundee University Scottish Nationalist Club. Two visits passed without raising any misgivings in my mind. On the third occasion, however, I found that Nationalist principles and arguments were not proving wholly acceptable. There was no heckling, no open disagreement, but as I left I was aware of cold, inhospitable faces. On my way to the station my host, who had held the post on the previous year as well, and with whom I thought I had a friendly enough relationship, said he would be leaving at the end of the session, but expected that I would be back again next year. I replied that I hoped so, and that I also hoped that his club would by next year have some Nationalists among its members. He looked slightly taken aback but didn't say any more. His name was Brian Wilson. What a future lay ahead of him and how he has vilified us over the years. I hope it wasn't something I said.

CHAPTER 7

DUNDEE WEST TO WEST FIFE

In May 1968 the Party's municipal candidates were successful to a degree which staggered everyone, friend and foe alike. Just how much of a mixed blessing this success was, is well-explained by Gordon Wilson (Chapter 6). In Dundee's 12 wards, the result in 11 of them was wholly predictable, given the social character of each. Only in Camperdown was the incumbent Labour councillor open to serious challenge. In the event, Tom McFettridge was elected as the Party's one councillor to sit for the next three years. His election brought sudden curiosity from the Press. It was my good fortune to be representing the Party in the Caird Hall's broadcasting, temporary, studio. I was asked one of these daft, lazy questions which have bedevilled Party spokespersons over many years. What, I was asked, would Mr McFettridge now seek to do? With what hopes of success? I gave the simplest of factual answers, that Tom was our only councillor, and with no seconder to support him, there were obvious limits to what he could achieve. He would, of course, be as good and active a representative of his ward as he could.

What immediately followed is barely credible. The local Party members, very properly, organised a social gathering to celebrate giving themselves the chance to enjoy their hard-won success. At its first meeting, perhaps, but certainly very soon after taking office, the new Council had voted that members should receive a medal which they and their families and descendants could own and cherish for years to come, if they felt like doing so. As we sat at our celebratory tea and sausage rolls, one man asked Tom if he would be taking his medal. I don't know if anyone else had bothered one way or the other, but Tom, without any apparent need for anxious and profound thought, said that he probably would. The questioner then, and for weeks, months and years thereafter, built and maintained a vendetta against this dreadful man who had betrayed us all and had cost the city some £12. It reminded me of the welcome extended to Robert McIntyre after his Motherwell success. Like Robert, Tom McFettridge was denied the chance, the right in fact, to take pleasure in his victory which was very much ours too. Instead this nonsense

86

about the medal never stopped, and meant that it became the done thing to run down Tom McFettridge.

The Labour Party reacted more wisely. Having lost the Camperdown Ward in 1968 to Tom, they were desperately afraid of losing it again in 1969 to our candidate, Dave Beattie. It was not, in Dundee, a mere matter of vanity. Control of the Dundee Council by the sad tradition of the time, was considered of great material benefit for that Party's councillors, their colleagues, their families, their friends. Local jests abounded, about Chicago councillors coming to Dundee on refresher courses or as a kind of finishing school. I wrote to Secretary of State Ross asking him to offer information and action to deal with some of the allegations. His response was the usual, "If you have any evidence….." etc.

Wishing to take no risks and to leave nothing to political chance, some persons in Labour's high places, now worked out how the SNP's hopes for another victory in Camperdown might be dashed. Tom McFettridge was employed by a small firm, whose owner simply could not afford to pay a new employee to help him while Tom was on Council business. With reasonable goodwill on both sides, Tom then looked around to find a firm with a bigger labour force, of the sort which employed many Labour councillors, all of whom had no difficulties in combining council duties with continued paid employment.

Tom swiftly found that, as one Labour councillor told him, "You're not on." So, step 1 of the plan was now in place. Mr McFettridge was unemployed and vulnerable. Step 2 was taken when Tom had it explained to him that Labour knew of his plight, and would continue to use it against him. Whereas, it was pointed out, a glorious future might be his if he would fall in with a few suggestions. If he did – "Two thousand a year, Tam, and a car." The alternative was increased descent into poverty. "They are ruthless bastards," said the emissary during the negotiating.

Then the favour being sought, which would bring such riches in return, was explained. Using his position as a leader of his Party's campaign he would be able to collect together SNP campaigning material. He was to do what he could to sabotage production of this material, but as some was bound to be produced he was to take charge of that, and take it over to Fife, where it would be handed over for destruction. Do all this, and then see what benefits you will enjoy. He indicated that he'd give his answer, and off went the go-between having carried out his masters' bidding.

Tom now made several contacts. He went to his priest. He then came to me, and together we arranged to meet with the two civic leaders of the time, Lord Provost Mackenzie and the leader of the administration, Mr Fitzgerald. These gentlemen brought in the Chief Constable, as I understand it, although I was not present at this later meeting. It was decided that the culprits would be allowed to betray their plot by having Tom, suitably equipped with microphone, arrange a meeting with the previous messenger. The co-operation of Dundee C.I.D. was offered, but turned down by McFettridge, on the grounds that detectives and Labour councillors were hob-nobbing nightly in the Arctic Bar. It was agreed, therefore, that an outside force be involved.

Thus the day arrived when three detectives from Glasgow came through to conclude the business. One of them was busy ostensibly repairing his car in the street, while his two colleagues were in the house monitoring events. All went according to plan. With incrimination on tape the luckless councillor was arrested for whatever definition of corruption the Fiscal might decide upon.

At the ensuing trial, Tom was fiercely grilled by Lord Ross, as he later became, at that time a court lawyer, a Dundonian himself, and frequently employed when needed by the Labour Party in the city. Tom's memory and determination remained unshaken, and Sheriff Margaret Kidd gave her verdict "Guilty on all counts", whenever Mr Ross sat down.

It might be thought that the Party would rally round after this courageous fight, but instead, members allowed themselves to be affected by Labour's suggestions that Tom was some sort of grass. Labour did expel the messenger, but his star eventually rose again. Several senior Labour figures, who may well have known something of this episode, some years later went on trial for corruption, but only two went to jail, and one was soon released following appeal.

While all this excitement was happening, the Party was turning its thoughts to the General Election of 1970. Tom had made up his mind that I should be candidate for Dundee West. I was less than enthusiastic. I didn't feel that I knew the city well enough at that stage, so I let matters drift as long as possible. However, the decision had to be made, and I agreed to nomination.

Of the wards in the constituency, Camperdown was the real base, and was obviously in support. Riverside was in friendly hands, Lochee, always thinking itself independent of Dundee, was friendly enough as long as they were allowed to follow their own reasons for whatever they did. Downfield had not recovered from its feud with Camperdown, so could not be relied upon. Law & Balgay each had a reasonable number of activists, which was good news in one sense, but unfortunately, it meant that they might stray as New Labour might put it, "off message".

The first row was needless. One of the Law members was an enthusiast for physical exercise and in particular, martial arts. He announced his wish to start, under SNP auspices, a karate class. Tom, for some reason, was wholly opposed to the proposal, perhaps fearing that it might mean more highly skilled violent men. Thus a fairly heated quarrel occurred.

While this simmered, we had a problem, not wholly unknown elsewhere, of a member of the Party taking out membership in two different branches, and, in this particular case, two different constituencies. It could be made to look like admirable enthusiasm, but in fact its effect would be to allow any such person to bring, through his membership, the power to influence, doubly, Party decisions. This too caused simmering animosity.

Most seriously, there came the day when in the window of SNP premises in the Hilltown, there was displayed a notice inviting signatures to a petition supporting the racial attitudes of Enoch Powell and another calling for the restitution of capital punishment. Tom was well aware of my attitude to both, and knew that to be a candidate in such surroundings, was out of the question.

He called into the rooms and asked for a change of heart and policy. He claimed he asked politely. They claimed he asked abusively. Whatever the truth, my role as candidate was never again mentioned, and the Constituency Association disintegrated. So very sad was the whole business that Tom's friendship with his two closest allies ended, and his co-operation with his hoped for successor, Dave Beattie, was also affected.

I see Tom McFettridge as a man very unfairly treated by the world. A man with formal education ending far below the potential of his mind, but none the less showing the judgement and intelligence of which that mind was capable. His ability to grasp significance and organise his thoughts accurately and quickly, was shown in his fierce witness box battle with the man who in time became Dean of the Faculty of Advocates and Lord Clerk Register of Scotland. He was let down shamefully by the entire Party apparatus and by his fellow-members in Dundee, who even today have little regard to his memory; the old, for whatever reasons they may have, the young, because they have no memory of such long gone events, and no curiosity which might prompt them to learn. I am only sorry that I could not be more effective in helping him, but that was because lots of people didn't much like me either.

Now that my contesting Dundee West was out of the question, I found that another constituency had been considering me as their preferred candidate. The main mover here was Peter Wright, whom I had first met in the mid 60s during branch and public meetings in Kirkcaldy and in Buckhaven. Peter had been the main activist in building up Party strength in Glenrothes, where SNP candidates were so successful in 1968 that serious problems followed. There has often been a risk that people whose intention was only to do the Party a good turn by standing, have unexpectedly been elected, landing themselves in great working or family problems. This had happened in Glenrothes, and Peter, as Group leader, had been left to endure the embarrassment caused by the resignation of several colleagues who realised that they simply could not combine council service with their other obligations.

Peter was a young man, defiantly cheerful and never inclined to retreat. In spite of the let-down following the elections, he continued to battle with his Labour opponents, led by none other than Henry McLeish. Peter was full of ideas and vigour, a folk music enthusiast who saw how valuable spreading such an interest could be to all Scottish causes – an awareness which nearly became effective a generation later. He organised on behalf of the branch, folk nights, in the Golden Acorn, which were well attended and were of value in building the Party's image. He and Marilyn were enthusiasts for Scottish literature and poetry, and worked to a fine balance of cultural and material politics.

Peter had decided that he wanted me to be candidate in West Fife. Feeling provisionally bound to Dundee, I also felt that, if I were to go back to Fife, it ought to be to Dunfermline. However, these avenues were no longer possible, so I agreed to come out of electioneering retirement and allow Peter to suggest me to his colleagues.

West Fife turned out to be the kind of constituency which a candidate finds rewarding. The variety of the communities was fascinating. Even in villages dependent upon mining, there were intriguing differences. No-one who moved around in them could even have confused Ballingry with Cardenden for instance; Kincardine was unlike either, as many of its residents would have been glad to arrange, and Aberdour was another world.

A key meeting with the officials one Sunday afternoon confirmed my adoption. All was very harmonious, but I saw, reading faces, two men with some doubts in their mind. Only after all was cut and dried did Peter gleefully confess what had been going on behind the scenes. One or two of his delegates had put forward the suggestion that winning the election was unlikely to say the least, and that greater publicity would be gained if the constituency chose, instead of a Party man, a real personality, whose presence would capture attention and enliven things generally for the whole Party.

It was a very valid point of view, and, if I had known, I could very well have gone along with it. However, the Constitution lays down that a candidate must have been a Party member for a prescribed period, and personalities from whatever source, were unlikely for that reason, to be eligible. So Peter had ruled, and pointed out the rule-book to the others, and they let their dream go, and settled for me instead.

What might have been! And how the West Fife survivors of those days must have had some wry smiles. The alternative candidate with whom I was in unknown competition was Sean Connery.

The most pleasing aspect of the campaign which followed was the way in which each community produced for us its quota of supportive workers. We started with an adoption meeting, which Winnie Ewing came to address, and every day saw our people working in their own areas while I spent most of each day in the area where our major evening meeting was to be held. Each sector of Glenrothes had to be visited, as well as the older established Leslie and Markinch. I met up with some of my students in Kinglassie and Cardenden, and in various Wemyss-es. In Kincardine, where Denholm and Myra Christie had built up a well-recognised presence for us, more help was provided by several of my former pupils from Dunfermline High. I found their presence and help especially rewarding.

In Kincardine at an early stage we were put under scrutiny by a Labour observer. We had expected a nasty campaign from Labour and Willie Hamilton, who had the reputation of playing the man rather than the ball. I imagine that his scout reported that I could not be written off convincingly as a Tory, and in the event I was spared anything like the malicious whispers which had attended some of Mr Hamilton's opponents on other occasions.

As in Stirling and Falkirk and Grangemouth, our members and supporters were very fine people and deserved a good result. And yet there was a nagging doubt in my mind. Looking back I now realise that in Scotland we were unaware of the swing to the Tories which had gathered momentum in England, and was to put them into government on polling day.

Polling day itself provides my abiding memories of West Fife. Starting in the morning in Cupar I paid what was a formal courtesy call on the local bureaucrat in charge of the management of the election. He did say, "Good morning," and swiftly followed with "Please remove that rosette." Later on, in Aberdour, sitting at her own table beside the polling staff, I found a very smart lady, royal blue from hat to shoes, and with a blue rosette the size of a pot lid. There was nothing new in finding one law for us and a different one for the party dominant in the area, but this was one of the finest examples of this recurring contempt for us and our very right to be competing at all.

It took hours to call at all the polling stations, and it was mid-afternoon before we made Crosshill. Messages had been coming in throughout the day from Joe Paterson, our champion in that village, to the effect that he had been intimidated and pressured by the Labour powers to such an extent that he had retreated from the school and was left by the gatepost, just on duty and no more.

Jim Thomson, my agent, and I entered the old-fashioned school premises, with a central hall, reached through the main door, and with individual class-rooms whose doors opened from the hall, and which were actual voting places. In the hall were trestle-tables, with tins of biscuits, bread-boards, and loaves, from which helpers were making sandwiches. At least one large kettle was boiling on some sort of portable cooker, and, busy-as-bees

93

Labour workers were welcoming voters and ushering them, arm in arm, to cast their votes.

I asked one of the polling clerks to direct me to the Presiding Officer, but was told that "she was lying down". I said that I wasn't surprised, but would like a word with whoever was in charge. While waiting for the Deputy Presiding Officer, we asked the Constable keeping order if he would see to having all these people and their gala equipment removed. He just gaped, because he was a local lad and no doubt thought all that he beheld was just normal. We had done enough to make it apparent that we were making trouble, and the happy chatter stopped, the stove was switched off, lids were put on biscuit tins, and muttered oaths and threats now began to swell around us.

The deputy lady appeared at this point, smiling brightly, and asking what "seemed to be the problem?" We gave her the gist of it and she looked over her shoulder at the now emptying hall, and said "But, they've gone!" We asked her to be sure it stayed that way and left along the narrow passage-way to the door, through a gauntlet of angry persons voicing displeasure. We made it to the car, and moved off just as Sam – as in "wait you till Sam gets here" – got here, jumping up and down with raised fists, and dust puffs under his pounding feet, just like the cartoons. "We're just assisting the public" he explained and shouted his abuse after us till we passed out of sight.

Just to be sure, I saw that word was sent to Sheriff Mowat in Dunfermline, and I was told later on that he had indeed come to see that all was as it should be.

I hadn't expected much joy in the result, but I was disappointed to see the hopeless and pointless Tory presence so well-rewarded. The best to be hoped for was that in West Fife some lasting benefits in experience and practice would be left behind for the future.

It was no comfort to learn as the results came in, that it had been a bad night for us all. In particular the loss of Hamilton, while easily enough explained, was still a blow, and Party morale was at a pretty low ebb as the media set about reporting on it all, now that it was all over.

On the following day we were rewarded with the perfect timing. As patronising glossing over the Party's very continued existence was the media's interpretation of the results, a sudden late newsflash reported that the Western Isles had returned Donald Stewart. We now had our first M.P. to be returned at a General Election, and we had the continuing status of a Party with a Parliamentary presence. Donald's personality seemed so gloriously to suit the occasion, that our recovery was able to begin before the impact of defeat had really time to register.

CHAPTER 8

INTO PARLIAMENT

The Party matured quickly during the early 1970s. Valuable and impressive new recruits came forward as events in the wider political world prompted them to set aside their former loyalties. From within our own ranks younger members were identifiable as having leadership potential. The NEC over which Billy Wolfe now presided seemed to me more at home with professional-level politics, in large measure because of the more sophisticated understanding of economic issues which Billy himself and Douglas Drysdale had brought to the Committee.

Also, Party members found plenty to do, with by-elections in Gorbals and South Ayrshire. Though in neither constituency did we enjoy many advantages, we had better prospects in the third contest which came about in, of all places, Stirling, Falkirk and Grangemouth. Times had changed in the decade since my days there, and very much for the better. We had a strong municipal presence, particularly exemplified by the Provostship of Robert McIntyre.

The Party's election planning had been mainly in the hands of Robert himself and Winnie Ewing, but Robert now took a back seat while we considered candidate selection. Local connections can work against as well as for, and some felt that Robert's local profile might offer less excitement and novelty than might a new personality. One of our new top level recruits was Isobel Lindsay, who in the Party was proving a positive rocket, rather than a mere rising star. Without visibly throwing her weight about, she was exerting powerful influence within the NEC, where, exceedingly well-informed , highly-educated in political matters, she particularly enjoyed the admiration and support of the Chairman.

Another possible choice, another able, brilliant young woman, was Margo MacDonald, and she too was seen as a possible choice.

Both had their supporters, but a majority of us, myself included, felt that with Robert on the spot this was not the most rational time to pass over his claim. I felt that to pass Robert by in his own town, in defiance of his high standing among its citizens, would be beyond the understanding of the electorate. To deny him this opportunity to fight for the cause to which he had devoted his life, would be as cruel as it would be unwise.

In the event Robert was selected, and the campaign which followed must have been a sore trial to him, just as it was deeply frustrating to the rest of us. By every dodge and device that cunning politicians could contrive, Labour smothered the campaign. They confronted us not at all. They publicised no meetings, published no daily statements, were nowhere visible around streets or at doors, and made no attempt to engage visibly with the public. The media seemed to take Labour's word for it that nothing was worth reporting and they withheld publicity from the whole election process.

Labour's stifling of discussion succeeded in delaying the impact upon the public of the news of oil discoveries in Scottish waters. Robert as candidate used oil-related information, but once Stirling was behind us, with a creditable 35% of the vote cast for Robert, the campaign for proper understanding of oil's political importance was entrusted to Gordon Wilson. As a well-trained lawyer he mastered his brief quickly and accurately, and under his supervision the "Scotland's Oil" campaign began to gather momentum.

At more or less the same time, the Party in Dundee enjoyed the great good fortune of having a group of talented and competent members coming forward together. This latest accession of strength was in the Dundee East constituency where they had developed the Broughty Ferry branch. How unusually lucky we were when the Dundee East M.P., Labour's George Morgan Thomson was going to be given a peerage and sent to Europe to speak for Britain.

Our constituency officials sought information about potential by-election candidates. Their inquiries prompted them to think particularly of two of the Party's better-known figures, Gordon Wilson and Margo MacDonald. To be frank, the specifically candidate-like skills seemed then to belong especially to Margo. She was an impressive public personality, loving the platform, comfortable in the limelight and splendidly at ease with company. Gordon's experience in so far as I knew it at the time, had been in organisation, administration, judgement of our best interests, and all these less demonstrative qualities. Partly for this reason I was not sure if he really wanted to be a candidate, happier rather to give the Party as a whole the benefit of his qualities. Fortunately the Constituency sought the guidance of the NEC, and their choice fell upon Gordon.

What followed was to me a revelation. The apparently cool, austere National Secretary turned out to be a campaigner every bit as street-wise as anyone. He and his local team began a programme of activity which would allow them to start the by-election with their machine already running smoothly. Gordon set himself a punishing schedule of his own professional work followed by evening dashes to Dundee where the ruthless locals had committed him to meetings, door-stepping and canvassing, and then he had to return home and be ready to do it all over again within a day or two. It was a remarkable performance, and it was rewarded, as it deserved to be, with the interest and growing respect of our own people first of all , and then, as time passed, of the wider public.

In March 1973 the by-election took place. Both our main rivals behaved predictably. The Conservatives were going to act the role of defenders of local interests. They nominated Lord Provost Fitzgerald, and spent time and money producing complicated posters faked up to look home-made. (It's a trick which affluent, propertied parties of the Right like to adopt. The Republicans in the U.S.A. were at the same nonsense recently).

Meanwhile Labour, with the blind partisan obstinacy to which they seem always prone, chose a candidate whose background made sense to them, but to no-one else. A Trade Union official from Sheffield was no doubt entitled to a safe Labour seat, somewhere, but hardly one so far from home. George Machin was, I am sure, a perfectly decent man, but his selection did prompt disbelief.

Unfortunately the nature of the contest was quickly complicated when Mr George McLean, our troublesome acquaintance of the 60s now decided that his qualities required him to compete. Calling himself the "Scottish Labour Party" he and his supporters took many more votes than anyone else might have expected. He found some support from disgruntled Labour voters who were unhappy with their Party's choice of candidate, but who felt disloyal at the thought of coming over to us in one move. I know that I was not the only Nationalist who felt that McLean's intervention was enough to deny Gordon the victory which was so near, and, as it turned out, not too long delayed.

With the excellent result in Dundee the Party fought its next contest, this time with Margo as candidate, in Govan. The local Labour Party was enfeebled, holding the seat just out of habit and lack of challenge. Margo changed all that, as she and her supporters galvanised Govan's – and Glasgow's – politics, while the Press and the public alike revelled in the excitement of the presence of the "glamorous", "blonde bombshell" as the media babbled in happy amazement. So Margo was elected and went off to give us a party of 2, joining Donald on his vigil.

In good heart we waited for the next election.

As an NEC member I had, of course, carried out whatever duties came my way. Gorbals andSouth Ayrshire saw me only on one or two campaigning days, but of course Stirling and Dundee were different and involvement was to be expected.

Also I was one of a delegation sent to meet with officials of the Common Market, whose maturing was going to require us to introduce ourselves to them and to inform them of Scotland's interests and opinions which we knew would never have been mentioned by British representatives.

Billy couldn't go, and sent George Leslie to head our group, Winnie Ewing, Douglas Crawford and myself. The official meeting was predictably odd. We were spoken to with total courtesy, but as though we were idiots who had to be told that "Well in Holland you see, we grow tomatoes, and of course you can't do that in Scotland." When we did try to show that we had some understanding of basic Political Economy, all the staff members were suddenly told to leave, and the politicians settled down to have an argument which they clearly intended would be very brief and very dismissive. The best part of the event was to meet in the house of an exiled Scots couple in Brussels, where I heard for the first time, Dougie McLean's song "The Lairdie's Prayer", which really ought to be revived on the Party's social occasions.

Round about, as branches and C.A.s had public meetings, I would go along, sometimes as NEC emissary, sometimes just as visiting or supporting speaker. Sharing the platform were usually colleagues well-known to me, but occasionally I met new acquaintances. On one such occasion I joined a gentleman of whom I had heard much admiring and respectful talk, especially in the Angus area. He was thought to be a very valuable accession to our ranks. His name was Viscount de Witt. As it happened during my student days I knew something of that family and its rivalry with the House of Orange, so I quite looked forward to our meeting.

The Viscount was the main speaker, and spoke calmly and quite sensibly, but did not seem to me to justify the degree of excitement which his arrival among our new members seemed to have caused. I wondered if some day I would be better able to understand.

Enlightenment came many months later when a court case was heard about misrepresentation of some sort, and the reports revealed that there was no such title in any peerage, British or Dutch, and that Viscount de Witt was in fact a sad chap who was a patient in a Montrose hospital, who had sought to comfort himself with an alternative personality.

Our work was put to the test when a General Election was called in February 1974. There was, as always, much ill-founded optimism around the country, but at least in Dundee we felt certain that having lost so narrowly in the by-election, Gordon Wilson was a virtual certainty to win now. By this time the SNP in Dundee East was formidably efficient, and Alan McKinney as agent and the C.A. team ran a campaign of such impressive competence that we were able to enjoy reports of visiting Labour dignitaries having to be looked after in their shocked condition until they felt ready to take up their schedules.

I spent Election afternoon and evening travelling through constituencies on behalf of the NEC, from one side of the country to the other. I have had few more thrilling boosts to my loyalty and confidence in our cause, than I enjoyed that evening as I crossed constituency boundaries one after the other. The names of the candidates on the posters changed as the miles passed, but at every boundary the black and gold colours met the eye. Dundee East, West, Perth, Kinross, Clackmannan, West Stirling, East Dumbarton, and then back through West Fife, Dunfermline, Kirkcaldy, East Fife and back home in time for the count. It was in West Stirling – Drymen – that, speaking for Janette Jones, I got the daftest question I have ever heard, from a barely-controlled furious Professor of Church History who shouted at us, "How may I ask, will you protect your oil-installations against the Chinese?" As a teacher I had long ago learned that the questions most difficult to answer were those that you never imagined anyone was daft enough to ask. Never mind the West Lothian question. Just imagine how to cope with Chinese troops in the North Sea.

In spite of the Professor's misgivings, as we all now remember, the Party won seven seats – a far cry from the days when we couldn't even contest more than two. The major disappointment was Labour's regaining Govan at Margo's expense. But Gordon was indeed elected. Donald held on comfortably, and Winnie returned to Parliament. John MacCormick's son Iain won the Argyll lands of his father. In East Aberdeenshire where the indefatigable Gordon Boyd had built an organisation which had already come close to electing Alex Farquhar, the Party strength was harnessed to elect Douglas Henderson. The other two were strangers in Party terms, having been active in other parties. It remained to be seen how successfully they would settle among their new colleagues, as people with previous experience in other parties often assume that the SNP is, in comparison, too naïve for its own good. They have not always been wrong.

CHAPTER 9

ELECTION COMMITTEE

The Party's Election Committee had been the responsibility of Winnie and Robert McIntyre. Now that Winnie was back in an active House of Commons role, and Robert was seen, principally, as a contact with the Group, the convening of the Election Committee now fell to me.

It was our job to identify possible candidates; assess them from references, and by interview, and organise training courses for those accepted. We met at least once a month and, as required, more often. The organisation's secretarial work was carried out by Helen Davidson who had wide experience as candidate, councillor and adviser upon whom Winnie and Robert had relied. No-one was more to be trusted than Helen. No-one was such a source of wise advice and sound judgement. As the first contact to whom aspiring candidates turned she gave the most encouraging and reassuring of welcomes, and the Committee benefited from the good relationships which she established right from the start of a candidate's career.

Robert remained as a member, as did Winnie, but other duties limited her appearances. A permanent member was David Rollo whose essential kindness did not prevent him arriving at shrewd assessments of applicants. He always asked each applicant what they had been reading and what they felt they had learned from their studies. Those few who had never felt the need to read anything, felt their inadequacies keenly after David's gentle scrutiny.

NEC members, especially those with particular responsibilities like Publicity, Organisation and so on, were usually present. Colin Bell was heroic in training candidates to face radio and TV interviewers. Jim Fairlie was very welcome to me personally, because he was of the austere and unyielding Nationalist persuasion, which suited me.

The Parliamentary Group nominated two of their number to be their eyes and ears and to bring the Group's advice to the Committee. The two sent were the two MPs who had come from parties other than our own – George Reid and Hamish Watt. Both gave most generously and responsibly of their time, and were especially active in urging us to act as swiftly as possible to provide a number of accredited candidates in time to give CAs a wide enough selection from which they could draw, as a Scottish devolved Assembly would require, suddenly, many more candidates than had been needed in the past.

Both men urged us to pick people of the strongest possible will. We need killers, they insisted. I was not too keen on their concentration on this quality, and once suggested that I'd want to know who or what manner of person our nominees would propose to kill? I felt that here in our own committee I had met persons who, having experience from within another party, felt that that party represented serious politics while the SNP was hopelessly amateur and naïve.

We all managed to rub along well enough. We met many people, able and honourable. Most, we were happy to recommend as candidates. Some we had to ask to find other forms of Party service. We had to assess abilities which were relevant, and we had to assess temperament, and guess at possible behaviour under pressure of public scrutiny. For some it would have been no kindness to choose them, and we did try to make people recognise that we were not passing judgement on their overall merits, but merely upon the particular relevant skills which were called for. Sadly, and inevitably, not all of them appreciated this, and I felt very sad to know that many good people had been hurt by our decision. I was able, with the Committee, "to see ourselves as others see us" when at one National Council Willie MacRae described candidates as being entrusted to "Jimmy Halliday's mincer." That's how it must often have seemed. I regretted it, but it couldn't be helped. If I could prevent it, the Party would never be shamed or embarrassed by any candidate who passed our tests.

Difficulties arose of course. There was an understanding that the Committee's decisions would be supported by the NEC, and we would not be required to explain our decisions, which sometimes depended upon confidential information and even warnings. We always checked and inquired, but on a few occasions we had to act upon this kind of information. As well as our own opinion in a candidate's suitability, we had to take into account the probable response of the NEC to any nomination we might make. It was with some apprehension that we sent forward the famous wealthy landowner and friend of royalty, Colin Tennant. He did not persevere in his quest for an SNP seat, so any possible dissension came to nothing.

On another occasion an NEC meeting in the Golden Lion Hotel in Stirling was interrupted by the arrival of two late comers, Gordon Murray and Bill Lindsay. Both were clearly very pleased about something and with themselves. It emerged that they had had an approach from a Glasgow Tory Councillor who was considering joining the SNP. Not only that but he was hinting broadly that his Party's MP for whom he worked, was also considering joining. The Councillor, Mr James Anderson, was in my view, a foolish populist Tory, whose most famous suggestion had been to place minor criminals in the stocks, to be set up in George Square. This proposal to restore 18th Century notions of law enforcement seemed so absurd as to disqualify its proposer from any serious consideration as a Party member, let alone a candidate. All public evidence suggested that his MP, Mr Edward Taylor, shared his outlook, and in my opinion was equally unthinkable. I was briefly alarmed to realise that some colleagues seemed to think that recruiting Teddy Taylor would be a clever thing to do. Again we were spared any internal troubles as Mr Anderson did not pursue his approaches, and Mr Taylor in due course was to threaten legal action against anyone who suggested that he had ever had any such intention as attributed to him.

One other little whisper of possible sensational recruiting came with the suggestion that Mr Jo Grimond, at the time sole Scottish Liberal MP, might condescend to join the SNP. Though only a whisper, Arthur Donaldson dealt with it by stating that any application by Mr Grimond would be considered as any other would be. He would need to understand however, that he would join as a member, and not as the new and newly-fledged leader of the SNP. So we heard no more of that one, and Mr Grimond was gradually given the comfort and reassurance of a few Parliamentary colleagues.

Only very late in the day did the NEC destroy the basis of our procedures, and only then because the NEC was disfiguring itself with dissensions, feuds and intrigues. As a result, candidates before the Election Committee were successful or not, depending, not upon the Committee's judgement, but upon the power of NEC members who were their personal supporters. Once this method of selection had begun, all nominations came to be decided by just another vote on the NEC where, by this time, votes were entirely predictable and personal preferences obvious and unchangeable.

Before we reached this stage, we had to deal with some problems which our leaders foisted upon us. Two of them landed me personally in the worst situation in my whole Party career.

In the summer of 1974, after February but before October, we had a National Council meeting in Govan. Before the meeting began, and while I was expecting to announce the names of adopted candidates, I was given a letter, in the name of the Parliamentary Group, asking the Election Committee to refrain from confirming the adoption of George Thomson in Galloway. George apparently had not fought the February campaign with the degree of ferocity wished for by the Group, who felt that they might suggest a future colleague more to their liking. I could not, without further discussion and investigation, ignore the request from the MPs and I had to arrange a hasty meeting with the Galloway delegates to tell them that George's adoption could not, at this stage, be announced.

They were bewildered and upset, angry no doubt, though they did seem to appreciate that the Committee was obliged to respond to the MPs' wishes. Fairly quickly we made our own checks, consulted with local opinion and decided that George's nomination would stand. It did, and he was elected, serving his constituency and Party well.

The second unpleasantness came about because the nomination of Derek Cameron in Kinross and West Perthshire proved to be unpopular with some parts of the organisation in the constituency. It was a row which neither I, nor any colleague, had seen coming, but the rival factions seemed irreconcilable.

No doubt in an attempt to make the Committee bring about a show-down, one of Derek's supporters phoned me, her purpose being to seek to discredit some of his opponents. As I have said, I was always anxious to save the Party from embarrassment arising from the deeds or public image of members, in particular, parliamentary candidates and their supporters. I was advised that some of the rival faction were not suitable or reliable in offering their opinions. To prove her point the lady made very hurtful and slanderous remarks about her adversaries. They were so rotten that when one of the rivals began to tell his tales of counter abuse, I stopped him, and urged him as a member, to realise what abusive depths he and his opponents alike were plumbing. I told him what had been said, assuming that he would be sufficiently shocked and ashamed, and would sober his campaign. I assumed that both sides would accept an obligation dictated by Party discipline and loyalty, to stop the vilification of colleagues.

I learned a hard lesson. Party loyalty is very feebly felt within the SNP, and if put under strain by factions of opinion, locality, personality, or any other, these other loyalties will win.

The man to whom I had made my appeal, did not, in shame, do what he could to end the malice. On the contrary, he told the slandered victims what had been said about them, and I found myself pressed to name the perpetrator. A phone call has no witness. Any accusation I might make would merely be denied and the dispute, even more vicious, would persist.

It took a long time and patient explaining before the affair was allowed to fade. In the meantime Derek Cameron became a candidate and came within a mere handful of votes of being elected. I did him further damage. At a meeting in Kinlochrannoch, I allowed myself, as supporting speaker, to lose my temper with a particularly superior and infuriating questioner, who then took offence and walked out. Having warned candidates over and over of the dangers of losing your temper, it was a very low point in my electioneering career.

CHAPTER 10

THE MAGNIFICENT SEVEN & THE FIRST ELEVEN

So we rejoiced in our success. It seemed the most amazing reversal of political fortunes, the most remarkable victory since trumpet blasts brought down the walls of Jericho. It was all barely credible and very wonderful.

There's always a snag. The constituencies which we had won all had very strong local identities which probably took priority in the minds of the voters over national issues. The economies of these areas did not provide useful insights into the problems, issues, and consequential thinking, of urban and industrial Scotland. I felt some uneasy memories of past Conference agendas and resolutions, dwelling upon such topics as the culling of stags and the problems facing hill shepherds. These were deserving of attention and action, but in the areas concerned there were few voters. Elections had to be concerned with the problems of the major population centres, and there we had made no captures. Dundee was indeed a city with urban problems, but it was fortunate in being free from the brutalities of the Clyde valley's class and sectarian wars. Some day, if we were to progress, we would have to challenge in these areas.

But we celebrated. The MPs, the NEC, the HQ officials all met for lunch in the Caledonian Hotel at the west end of Princes Street. Billy presided, and harmony reigned. Then, back to business. Douglas Henderson, selected as Whip of our Group, rose and pushed back his chair. "Will all those who have been elected follow me please," and he marched smartly through the door behind him. I do believe that some of the MPs looked a bit sheepish as they did as he asked, but the effect on some who remained was clear, and the effects of that incident were long-lasting and damaging, underlying animosities which revealed themselves in years to come.

Our problem was that we had not elected the most appropriate people. We did not elect Billy Wolfe or Margo MacDonald or Isobel Lindsay or Willie MacRae. If we had done so our progress since would have been swifter and more complete.

Instead the Party's leading personalities were now separated by the roles which they had to play. There is too often a tendency to be over-theoretical in making policy or deciding tactics, whereas realities dictate outcomes. When we had two MPs, they were, as it were, scouts in alien territory and Party power lay beyond all doubt, back home in HQ with the NEC. If we were to have, say, 30 MPs, the importance of the NEC would be negligible and HQ merely a depot from which the Parliamentary party was served. All very obvious really. But what about when we have seven MPs? How important are they? How strong should they be in our decision-making? Whose will prevails – theirs or the NEC's?

Holyrood has given us the answer to this, as to so much else. We have 69 MSPs, and I for one don't even know who the NEC members are. I don't think I'm alone. And if any NEC partisans want to argue the toss about balance of power, let them remember that branches and CAs, and the voters whom they represent, will support their MP or MSP against any NEC, and with 40 times each branch and CA delegate entitlement, an NEC trying to impose its will can go whistle.

Sadly, with 7 MPs things were not at all decisive. On political issues, MPs from our constituencies found themselves out of agreement with NEC members from cities and industrial towns. The NEC wanted to appeal to voters in places where we had lost, where Labour ruled, and where we were drawn into competition, trying to out-do Labour at their own game.

It was clear that Labour would call another election to secure a more decisive result, and so we came to the October election. We had, as a Party, really used the time quite well. Our MPs had a good enough image in the eyes of the general public, and we had done our best to keep ourselves fully ready and prepared as far as our resources would permit.

Our reward was to win four more seats, and send four more colleagues to the House of Commons. The near misses of February became victories in October in Angus, Perth and East Perthshire, and Galloway. A finely-balanced 3-way contest saw Margaret Bain snatch East Dunbartonshire from the puzzled big battalions. And once again we were encouraged to celebrate. After all, we had won more seats, had we not?

At various times in history, (a very difficult thing to explain), we find that timing is vitally important. This was one such moment. Pressure, tension, built up for Labour and ourselves all through the middle months of 1974. Labour saw themselves as needing to crush us, while we saw ourselves as on an almost inevitable march to further success. But our 4 new MPs represented such a modest advance, that Labour knew they had seen off our challenge. Public opinion, which had begun to expect progress from us, now reverted to the usual opinion that we would never get anywhere.

Luck didn't smile upon us in one sense. We had no by-elections to allow us any display of sustained or refreshed challenge until April 1978. By that time, events controlled by others had weakened our prospects beyond hope of recovery when the next General Election came in 1979.

Labour's introduction of devolution proposals in itself cooled down much Nationalist excitement, while we waited in happy confidence for great things to happen.

The rest of the story can be followed in many books, but best informed for us is the narrative in Gordon's book. The long months of delay and evasion; the wilful muddle over how to treat Scotland and Wales, together or separately; the sheer boredom and loss of time provided by debating tricks in the Commons, and finally the realisation that the Labour Party would not support the passing of the Bill which its leaders had offered, left our Parliamentary prospects in ruins.

Our success had seemed to endure until 1977, when an election seemed inescapable, and we seemed likely to do well. Unfortunately, the Liberals at that precise moment had to avoid an election at all costs. Their then leader was under investigation and facing probable charges of having been involved in a conspiracy to murder. Small wonder that David Steel, his later successor, led his party into the sheltering arms of Prime Minister Callaghan who also had every reason to avoid an election which he would lose.

It has to be admitted that we did, some of us, bring much of the disaster upon ourselves.

CHAPTER 11

THE PARLIAMENTARY GROUP AND THE NEC

As the months passed, a goodly number of candidates were approved, and CAs began to organise their selection processes. We met, usually in the Cowane Centre in Stirling, but sometimes in more luxurious surroundings. On one weekend, for instance, we – Committee members and applicants alike – enjoyed the 5-star facilities of Culloden House Hotel, as guests of Kenny MacLennan, its owner. This outstandingly generous hospitality was the most lavish benefit which I have ever received as a result of my Party involvement.

The secretarial work, correspondence, filing and minuting, was all done by Helen Davidson who also helped me to remain reasonably calm at most times. The main pressure, to move swiftly and process large numbers, came at each meeting, from our MP colleagues. Without disagreeing with their pleas of urgency, I did what I could to make sure that we did not allow our standards of selection to drop. I also came to believe that the MPs were impatient at having to await decisions from amateurs like us, thus causing delays to professionals like them. Knowing what I did of the personalities involved, I was all too aware that any impatience displayed by George and Hamish would be equalled if not surpassed, by that felt by, especially, Douglas Henderson who was temperamentally irritated by any undue time spent by persons less quick-witted than himself. There was, in this one committee, an example of a growing problem. The MPs, or some of them, were beginning to show signs of talking down to their Party colleagues, including the NEC.

Any group of people elected to important positions, and carrying out their functions under the gaze of media and public, can become very conscious of their fame. To the outsider they will very possibly appear to be arrogant, to see themselves as an elite. The members of our Parliamentary Group were far too varied in temperament to think of themselves as an elite. But they had been elected, after all, and could be forgiven for assuming that their own personal excellence had given them their victories.

In the opinion of others, the credit belonged to the Party workers in the constituencies concerned. So due credit and admiration was sometimes grudged.

If arrogance was a possible defect among the Parliamentarians the damaging emotion on the NEC was jealousy. The insensitive assertion of special status on the occasion of that first celebratory lunch was not forgotten. Gordon tells us that Billy claimed to have forgotten the episode. What I remember very clearly was the stricken expression with which he observed the upstanding and departure of those whom he had led, while he himself had to remain. With emotions of superiority and jealousy in play there was every temptation for Group and NEC to minimise the status of each other. Gordon quotes a remark by Margo MacDonald which he describes as "close to insulting, and intended to be so". I would totally agree with him on both counts.

To these various personal animosities time brought added grounds for strained relations between the two bodies. For some reason which was never really studied, the divergence between "gradualists" and "fundamentalist Nationalists" reasserted itself, as gradualism came to be the chosen methodology of the Left.

Outwith the Party, in the wider political world, Nationalism was viewed with distaste by Socialist theorists. Its presence as an ingredient in Fascism, greatly emphasised and publicised by Labour for their own electoral purposes, did raise doubts in many minds. Even in the 1970s the old division between Nationalist and Home Ruler still smouldered. Home Rulers were ready, even quick, to seize upon Labour's offer of devolution, which now began to be discussed. For them this was now to be the probable, best and preferred way forward. Winning a Westminster mandate was a fantasy. Not only was a new strategy available to us; it was right for us to move away from arguments aimed at winning recognition of Scotland's identity, to focus instead upon arguments aimed at "securing the best and fairest way of ensuring a fair deal for ordinary Scottish people/workers and their families" as Margo MacDonald put it.

So the potentially effective election-directed oil campaign was allowed to command less of our rhetoric, and our public image came ever more closely to resemble that of Labour in the country. Gordon records (Chapter 11 – "Fault Lines"), the several clues, hints, statements, admitted or denied, by Margo, claiming that the SNP was "a Socialist party, slightly Left of Centre" or "part of the Labour movement".

Sitting at NEC meetings while these sentiments were in the air, and knowing that the Parliamentary Group was far from wholly supportive of these opinions, I felt great regret that issues were being forced with unnecessary haste towards unpredictable consequences. As a student I had spoken as one of three Nationalist speakers in the 5th Centenary Debate in Glasgow University's Bute Hall. I spoke in support of a motion in favour of the Social Democratic position in politics. I meant it then, and in 1974, and for that matter, in 2010. But vital in my opinion was the word "Democratic". Socialism which disregarded, by-passed or rejected democracy was not to be favoured. As for "slightly Left of Centre" I wish I had cash for every time I heard one of our top brass use that term. It is a silly term. It means something only to political anoraks, and nothing at all to the less obsessive voters. "Radical" was another favourite and it too was a fatuous over-educated favourite. Many who love the word forget that "Radical" can mean something on the Right.

The trouble in those days, in England as well as here, was that "Socialism" had become a lazy word. It was used as if to imply just being nice to folk; vague, well-meaning and helpful. I tried as often as I remembered quickly enough to ask people who used "Socialism" as a term of praise just what it meant to them. I recall only one person having the pugnacity and honesty to meet my challenge. Margo explained that Socialism for her meant "a massive extension of public ownership and a punitive level of taxation". I have never forgotten the occasion. I know she was not joking, though how far she expected success for her programme I am not sure.

Socialism, as thus defined, cannot co-exist with democracy because people simply will not vote for that. Think of 1983 and Labour's so-called "suicide vote" manifesto which saw the party crushed. Or think of the Bennite programme, favouring a "siege economy". That had worked out while liberties were set aside during the war with all its restrictions and prohibitions. It could not work while opinions were free and unthreatened by invasion and conquest.

However, this kind of feeling hung over all NEC meetings. As we worked through the agendas, on every issue calling for decision Margo spoke, Isabel Lindsay spoke, Tom McAlpine spoke, Willie MacRae spoke, and on the next issue they all spoke again. The rest of us could have gone home, and perhaps should have done so, because meetings habitually went on until the small hours of the morning. Billy told me that he enjoyed these long discussions, and he expressed to me his anger that when Gordon became Chairman the time was more strictly controlled.

I was often in agreement with this dominant group, sometimes against. Similarly uncommitted among the frequently elected NEC members were Colin Bell, Jim Fairlie and Helen Davidson and, when present, Margaret Bain.

It became evident that the Parliamentary Group also had its divisions. The press began to talk of the "Gang of Four", by which they usually meant Douglas Henderson, Hamish Watt, Douglas Crawford and Winnie Ewing. Andrew Welsh, Margaret Bain, George Thomson and Iain MacCormick were less type-cast. Gordon, as I have told him, was most understanding among all the MPs, of the NEC's position. Very right and proper, for a former National Secretary of the Party, George Reid, though I did not know him personally at all well, I agreed with in his opinions more closely than with any other MP. George after all had Social Democratic credentials too.

CHAPTER 12

STRATEGIC DISAGREEMENTS 1979 – 1982

In the elections to the NEC in 1979, Conference delegates revealed a reaction against the strategy which the previous regime had pursued. Gradualism, balancing of the pros and cons of devolution; concentration on material comfort of the mass of the people – these had characterised the thinking of the most influential members of the NEC. The new NEC seemed to suggest that members favoured a return to more Nationalist attitudes. Perhaps so; but if so, that reaction did not last long.

With the formation of a group styling itself the "Interim Committee for Political Discussion", and in the absence now of a strong Parliamentary Group, NEC policy returned to the kind of programme which had been only briefly interrupted. The new Committee, soon to be known as "the '79 Group", was first mentioned to my knowledge, by Gavin Kennedy, an academic Political Scientist, with a lively line in argument. At its heart was Margo MacDonald, supported by various colleagues, notably Andrew Currie, who was once upon a time an adolescent supporter of the 55 Group. From the Right then, Andrew had moved to the Left now. Another influential member was Stephen Maxwell, once a professional official of the Party, but now an elected member. His experience gained in Headquarters meant that he was most knowledgeable in the management and administration of the Party affairs. His own academic credentials were widely appreciated, and he and Isobel Lindsay were constantly identified as "the Party's intellectuals" by the media. Though Billy Wolfe, Isobel, Tom McAlpine and Willie Macrae were powerful enough to pursue their own paths, they were on the whole sympathetic to the plans of the Group.

Gordon covers the events which followed (Chapter 18?) and explains how difficult things became for him as Chairman.

I was slow to appreciate disagreements. Not only did I support the general economic and social objectives of the Group, but I assumed that the Party collectively did so too. All through the years I had assumed that our anti-Unionist, anti-Imperialist stance placed us without any doubt on the political Left. Some individuals did puzzle me a little sometimes, but I never felt that the Party was likely to drift into anything like the "Tartan Toryism" of Labour's lying and ignorant mythology.

So I was taken aback to find that this new pressure group apparently felt it necessary to find grounds for an internal trial of strength within the Party. To promote their programme they declared themselves, not just a group, but "a Group", and proceeded to behave as such bodies must. They soon made a point of dividing the Party into "we" and "you", "us" and "the rest". As time passed, very quickly "you" became "our" rivals, opponents, adversaries. "You" do not meet with "our" approval because "we" are right, and "you" don't see things as "we" do. This constant emphasis on differences can never fail to provoke disunity, mutual dislike, and urge to drive opponents to impotence. It is certainly never a recipe for co-operation and harmony.

As time passed this new exciting mood spread to all levels of the Party. In advance of Conference and National Council, influencing of agendas was schemed and prepared, slates of candidates were chosen and promoted for all elections, and activists in the new cause evangelised among CAs and branches always with the aim of controlling Conference and thereby the Party.

At virtually all meetings, at whatever level, symptoms of disunity were on display. Secrecy of manner, furtiveness, guarded suspicion imperfectly concealed became normal and overt dislike was obvious.

As this poison spread through our ranks, Gordon asked me to take on the role of constituency chairman. I thought this idea was a mistake. We had already learned that the Party went through phases of hostility to anyone in office. Dundee East was not the worst affected by this blight, but I knew that neither Gordon nor I was a favourite with those members who had shown themselves to be sympathetic to the '79 Group. As an ex-teacher I was already resented by some anyway, and before long other evidence of antagonism showed itself.

An attempt was made to remove from membership one man on the grounds of his views on South Africa. When I ruled that we had no powers to take any such step, there was some displeasure shown by those who felt that mere constitutional rules should not protect those who held unpleasant opinions.

In this dispute the lead was taken by a man of experience whose commitment to the '79 Group came as a surprise. He was true to his principles because he was later instrumental in persuading SNP councillors to support the Labour nominee as Convenor of Tayside Region, totally indifferent to the fact that the nominee was also Labour's chosen opponent to face Gordon at the next election. The publicity and public status granted to him played some part at least in ensuring Gordon's defeat. This event seemed to me a measure of the animosity which now afflicted me.

From another branch official there came one of these insults to the intelligence to which brazen troublemakers are prone. With hypocritical concern we were asked at the C.A. to support a motion which would force Gordon to abandon either his seat in the House of Commons or the Chair of the Party. Also this was proposed in order to give poor over-worked Mr Wilson some relief! In response I expressed the hope that Gordon would suggest what should be done with the advice, and the matter was carried no further.

Meanwhile, I had been for decades a member of the Board of the Scots Independent. Politicians on any extremes have always disliked any publication which they did not control. Lenin had spread his revolutionary ideas from his Swiss exile by illegally distributing his magazine "Iskra" ("The Spark"). In most countries the Socialist parties had journals which shared, in their various languages, the same name. "Vorwaerts" in Germany; "Avanti" in Italy and "Forward" in Britain, all preached the message and words taken with the most devout seriousness by their supporters. The S.I. for various good reasons, was not owned by the Party, but was controlled by a private company, giving full support to the Party none the less. The S.I. was often unpopular precisely because it was not passing to and fro between rising and falling factions.

As the '79 Group grew in strength and in ambition its organisers asked the S.I. to carry an advert for its next major recruiting meeting. Editing the paper at that moment was Robert McIntyre. Robert had many times found himself under attack because of the stance of the paper. In 1955 the then dissidents attacked the S.I. as "the McIntyre Press". He now, as editor, advised the Board that in his view the advert was intended to advance a faction which he was not inclined to encourage. With one other supporter I moved that we should accept the advert. I felt the same kind of unwillingness to strike an attitude which would do more harm than good, as led me to oppose the overwhelming wish of the Party to vote for the "No Confidence" motion which brought down Callaghan. I believed then, and I believe now, that we did ourselves dreadful damage, needlessly. Now I saw the S.I. make the same mistake. And indeed the majority on the Board earned the enmity of the '79 Group, which, once its leaders were making decisions for the Party, made great difficulties for the paper from then onwards.

At much the same time the S.I.'s editor, Colin Bell, resigned in despair because he felt unwilling to offer the sort of couthy, parochial news which a survey of opinion seemed to support. It was not the case, and mature discussion was intended to clarify our purposes, but Colin left us without an editor. We had emergency editors at various times in the past, but now we needed to try to find someone who might stay for a reasonable time.

I knew from student days that in Glasgow there was an activist, ex-Parliamentary and Council candidate, Kenneth Fee, who was well able to tackle the task. He was invited to become editor, and in the event he stayed for 20 years. His skills and deep commitment to the S.I. earned him the gratitude of all who were responsible for the paper, and of all its readers over those years.

Unfortunately, he had been busy in and around Glasgow, attending '79 Group meetings, asking awkward questions, revealing embarrassing decisions and generally making a nuisance of himself. It probably would not have altered our decision, but although it was not at all our intention, his appointment was seen by the '79 Group as a provocation which, when added to Robert's refusal of the advert meant that the S.I. was a target for the hostility of powerful enemies.

In one last way the S.I. fell foul of prominent SNP figures. Gavin Kennedy and Colin Bell had an on-going kind of game involving the exchange of sharp comments and jibes between themselves and with Isobel Lindsay and Tom McAlpine. It was all very much a case of mutually tolerated badinage, or so the outside world thought. In one report in the S.I. some reference, I thought intended to be jocular, had been made to Isobel's political attitudes before she joined the Party. Nothing was said and no complaint was made until years later, at a National Council meeting in Largs, the S.I. was coming under fierce attack from various spokespersons from the Group. When I rose to answer the charges I found myself facing Tom and Isobel in the front row. It was the only time in my life that I have seen Isobel showing anger. As such a competent thinker, debater and presenter of arguments she was always in full good-humoured control. Her visible fury astonished and bewildered me. It emerged that in that long past paragraph, something was written which Isobel, and Tom on her behalf, found offensive. Their attack on me now was, that the S.I. had never apologised. This was wholly true, because no-one had any inkling that an apology was called for or desired. Nevertheless the anger on display that day revealed an alarming reservoir of pent-up dislike.

Conferences in Rothesay in 1980 and Aberdeen in 1981 saw the influence of the '79 Group growing steadily. As if to reinforce its strength it now promoted the Socialist Society, in which Socialist members of the SNP could make friendly common cause with Socialists in other organisations.

Anyone needing to learn how matters developed must read Gordon's narrative. He analyses the programme now advocated by the NEC in spite of his own reservations as "a magnificent exercise of cussedness and isolationism". This was the brief hey-day of "the Scottish Resistance" and civil disobedience. This kind of over-excited imagery and language simply did not fit the political realities in our country. We might sometimes wish that they did, and that Scots felt themselves occupied and conquered, but they do not, and the verbal fireworks just became so much windbagging. One leaflet produced to spread the idea of a Scottish Resistance, bore the silhouettes of figures waving clenched fists in the air. David Rollo always referred to their design as "the football hooligans leaflet".

As well as the '79 Group, now increasingly on the ascendant, there was the kind of amateur dramatic approach to politics practised by the Siol nan Gaidheal. Their misdeeds lay in their liking for military seeming regalia, with banners and arm bands, and a drum corps, all of which persistently displayed itself at demonstrations hosted by the Party. Our officials sought to deter them but they refused to be deterred.

Their behaviour brought the Party to a brief consideration of the problems posed by Groups, and an attempt was made to resolve matters at a National Council meeting in Arbroath. Gordon, in his own memories and also quoting Jim Fairlie, tells the disgraceful story of that day when two extreme factions made common cause against the moderate centre. One possible guide to our dealings with them was perhaps suggested when, as we considered the rival merits of Siol and '79 Group, Billy Wolfe laughingly revealed that he had joined both.

A victim of all these events was Alan McKinney. His promotion from being Gordon's election agent to becoming National Organiser was opposed then at the NEC, by Mrs MacDonald. Now that her star was in the ascendant Alan's prospects were bleak. He was first humiliated by being passed over for the post of HQ Director which went instead to one Iain More. When Mr More, a very mobile professional moved on, Alan combined the functions of HQ Director and National Organiser. Unhappiness over his conditions and his treatment eventually prompted his departure from the Party's service. By then (1990) the NEC was incapable of showing him courtesy let alone friendship, and it was a group of us as private individuals who met at a dinner in Alan's honour. They were the best of colleagues for Alan and for myself – Margaret Ewing and Fergus; Colin Bell, Helen Davidson, Jim Fairlie – a group which trusted one another and served the Party and our cause well.

As well as these tensions within the Party, and my increasing alienation from its leaders, events in the wider world were wearing down any enthusiasm. I had served for a brief period as the Party's External Affairs Convenor. It was not a success. I incurred Gavin Kennedy's scathing criticism because having suggested that he might serve on his Committee I then did not pursue the invitation. I did not discuss the matter any further with him at the time, because, again, internal disagreements were at work. I agreed with Dr Kennedy's views on Defence and diplomacy but I realised that his appointment would have provoked a sulphurous response from the Pacifists and CND zealots who were in the majority.

Finding myself for all these years in disagreement with the Party's policies on Defence and Foreign policy wore me down. I grew increasingly tired of the nursery-like attitude of colleagues who approached world problems with solutions offering pieties and crossed fingers. I grew tired of being anti-everything real and familiar and logical. The Party was in its public attitudes, hostile to Western Europe our historically cultural partners, while striving for affection from the Communist world. When Tom McAlpine in particular would make one of his recurring speeches in favour of "non-alignment", I knew, even if he did not, that in effect he was merely wanting us to change sides in the Cold War. Disarmament on the lines so often then urged would have had, as its first consequence, the conceding of initiative to the Soviet Union. When you are far enough away from its consequences, or have some strength and influence, then non-alignment might be feasible. It was a possible policy for India, for Egypt, for Yugoslavia, but not for our small, unfree little toe-hold on an island dominated by a superior power. If it was ever a serious argument it was an absurd one, but rather than have more rows, no one argued.

In its simplest form, the most wearing of all these irritants was the almost knee jerk display of hostility to America. There is the USA, greatest of all influences upon our popular culture, dominating our reading and our viewing, and influencing our citizens who assume friendship as a natural consequence. Instead our statements were increasingly of a piece with the utterances of these who made denunciation of America and its conduct a matter of daily comment. This gradually led me to wonder why I should remain an active servant of the Party capable of such unfair and unwise judgements.

Meanwhile my role as Dundee East C.A. Chairman was becoming increasingly unpleasant. I had to accept that the really active members did not share my opinions. At each meeting there was sure to be some initiative or motion which had been processed at a meeting of the Socialist Society on an earlier date. National Councils had the same experience. I remarked to David Coutts who wanted a lift to a National Council meeting in Stirling, that he had a cheek wanting me to help him to go along to try to get delegates to vote for whatever it was they had been told to do at their previous Socialist Society meeting. David laughingly accepted my complaint.

These pressures, and the hopelessness in trying to counter them prompted me to resign from my C.A. post. I kept it quiet for a time to allow Gordon to take whatever action he felt might help, and after a week or two revealed my intention. I had warned Gordon that he was going to have to fight his next election with the help of his personal supporters rather than the Party organisation. In fact, that organisation in its determination to display total rejection of the Tories, had placed John McAllion, Labour's candidate in the Regional Council chair. When asked why they had not consulted Gordon, the answer was "Why should we?" That really says it all.

CHAPTER 13

DIVISIONS AND DECLINE

Because the SNP has had some important successes in by-elections we are tempted to take it for granted that by-elections always work to our advantage. "Often" perhaps, but "always" unfortunately not. By 1977 the long drawn out Parliamentary swindle which deciding on Scottish devolution had become, was well underway. The pact between the Labour government and the Liberals had preserved Labour in office, had prevented the Liberal Party from disintegrating in ridicule and disgrace, and had denied the General Election in which all the indications were, that the SNP would do very well. Once again that moment, vital to our advantage, had passed, and by 1978 we were already over-the-top in any measurement of our strength and political success.

So, the by-elections which now suddenly happened were just too late to bring us maximum benefit. Hopes were still high when the Garscadden by-election was called in April 1978. This proved to be an event dramatic, significant and full of lessons for us.

It was assumed then, that parties in a hopeless position, would go in for "second-preference" voting, and vote for the party which had the best chance of defeating the most disliked opponent. The Tories in Scotland were a bedraggled dispirited bunch, and it was assumed that, in Garscadden, Tory voters would vote SNP to defeat Labour. Instead, obstinate and defiant work by Teddy Taylor, the much ridiculed but stubborn conscience of mean-minded, populist, West of Scotland Toryism, rallied the ranks. With the brazen vigour which we later came to know so well, Ian Lawson led the Tories in the constituency to secure a vote much higher than any observer had thought possible.

Some of the SNP laughed at Labour's selection of Donald Dewar as their candidate. Dewar, gawky, untidy, geeky, as far removed from working-class stereotype as could be, seemed an almost comical figure in the eyes of many of our members. Unfortunately, Labour working –class people formed a different impression.

125

Our campaign showed up many defects, the greatest being the refusal of our local leaders to co-operate effectively with the plans of the National Organiser. Whose idea it was to cast Garscadden as victim of Glasgow's municipal Labour Party got the facts wrong. Time and effort was spent in expressing furious concern for the most deprived areas in the constituency, although anyone with any political awareness would have known that the percentage vote in such areas would be tragically small. Meanwhile our canvassers were strenuously visiting housing estates of older vintage, assuring the tenants that they were suffering dreadfully at the hands of Labour. In those tenements not one dropped sweetie-wrapper caught my eye on any canvass trip. The afternoons saw a steady excursion of affluent-seeming ladies, smart and groomed, en route to the city's shops and entertainments. In due course they marched up to the ballot boxes and gave their votes to the Labour Party with which they felt perfectly satisfied.

My prediction about the likely outcome was founded on my knowledge of voting history in the United States, where the evidence beyond doubt proved that the greater the deprivation the lower the vote. I ventured this advice at an NEC meeting on a later occasion, to be reprimanded by Mr McAskill who put it that "Jimmy Halliday says the working class don't vote." This rather rough and ready approach to accuracy was quickly challenged and withdrawn. But the attitude of mind, refusing to reflect constructively, was disturbing.

Finally, Garscadden brought to the fore, a problem which has given the Party problems, and which it has not really understood let alone confronted.

Every study of Garscadden has considered as vital the selection of the SNP candidate, especially in that particular constituency. Keith Bovey was and is a man of great character, utterly honest and self-less, without being in the least naïve. But among his many qualities he was, and is, a man of principle. He was, and is, never going to conceal his principles or fail to act upon them. Those are admirable attributes.

The trouble is that high principles prompt a high degree of commitment. We are all committed in our various ways, to Scottish independence. Is that our highest political commitment? We manage, most of us perhaps, to see politics in practical terms, while our moral attitudes, just as with religious opinions, exist on a different plane. Unfortunately, in modern times moral principle has come to inhibit political behaviour. Our candidate had deep pacifist convictions and a particular commitment to the campaign for Nuclear Disarmament. This was going to allow Labour supporters to frighten the many voters whose wages depended on defence contracts providing work within the constituency. We all, then, since and right now, are entitled to our opinion as to whether or not we chose the appropriate candidate.

I once talked over this whole matter with Billy Wolfe who shared Keith's views. I argued that humanity must be placed higher than democracy, but that both must be guaranteed before we embraced Nationalism or independence. Pacifism, however, I would not place above independence. Billy claimed that he was not a Pacifist, though I could not quite understand where he drew the line.

He and many others revered CND, and encouraged closer ties between that organisation and the SNP. The argument was that SNP participants in CND activities would give us influence over CND policies. My own view was, and remains, that it rather gave CND great influence over our policies.

I once asked Isobel Lindsay how she would vote at a General Election if she had to choose between a candidate of another party who supported CND and me, who did not. She claimed that she would vote for me. I did not believe her then or now. In fact it seems to me that anyone who rejects CND has as much chance of a hearing in the SNP as an atheist has of election to public office in most states of the U.S.A.

Garscadden showed the possible unfortunate consequence of two convictions, sincerely held, requiring a decision between them.

In May there swiftly followed a by-election in Hamilton to be contested by Margo MacDonald. But even within that one month, the blow to our morale at Garscadden made our slump more rapid. At the time I remember being alarmed and puzzled by Margo's own apparent lack of enthusiasm for the contest. Gordon goes far to making us understand much of what the growing animosities were doing to damage us and diminish zest for the fight. The preoccupation now, at the highest levels of the Party, was increasingly with controlling the public image of the Party and its policies. Power to take these decisions meant competing within the Party, and that competition was now capturing the energy of prominent persons in the NEC and in the Parliamentary Group alike. Ill-will between them was a matter for discussion at all NEC meetings of the time, much fomented by Margo's reports of her visits to London.

The entire strength of the SNP throughout the years of its existence had been fully committed in the fighting of any by-election. Money was required from every member, branch, and constituency. Help in all elections – directed work, leafleting, canvassing, envelope filling, was required from every SNP body. Perhaps the growth by the 1970s had reduced the understanding of these simple facts.

Another simple fact, once widely understood, was that the entire Party was affected by the election result. Members gained pleasure from a good result. Enemies gloated over our defeats. The election was everyone's fight, everyone's task, was fought by us all and was funded by us all. It was therefore, I thought, appreciated by all members that a by-election would be planned and organised on behalf of the entire Party by the proper constitutional authority, the National Executive Committee and its agents. If a candidate brought adverse publicity of any sort, the entire Party would suffer. If a candidate was shown to be in any degree inadequate to the task, lacking in political knowledge or campaigning common sense, the entire Party would be disadvantaged. We all stood or fell together, and our national leadership should have the responsibility and the power to control the campaign.

At Garscadden these facts had been either ignored, rejected or simply forgotten, and local leaders asserted their supremacy over the National officials. The bad feeling was to some extent responsible for our defeat.

For those of us with responsibility for elections, there was naturally a determination not to allow the same thing to happen again. These considerations influenced us when we were faced with the by-election in Berwick and East Lothian following upon the death of Labour's John P. Mackintosh.

By this stage we had managed to compile a list of possible candidates in readiness for any elections in the near future, whether for Westminster or for a future devolved Assembly. Constituencies had begun selecting possible candidates from that list, but all such selections were made with General Elections in mind. Indeed every candidate on the list had signed a declaration that he or she understood and accepted that provisional selection did not mean automatic selection as candidate in a by-election. The pledge was included precisely because a by-election would involve full national press attention, and the choice of candidate would have to be made with that degree of exposure and scrutiny in mind. Our Party would be fully judged by the performance of this one individual. It was our duty and our right to select a person whom we thought informed and experienced enough to cope with this especial pressure.

As it happened, as we conducted our interviews and training sessions we had spent some time in committee deciding whether or not to place on the list of possible candidates quite a number whom we felt capable of being a one in seventy-odd General Election candidate. We were not at that stage called upon to assess anyone for by-election potential.

One candidate, accepted with many doubts and reservations, was one William Paterson. He seemed a very quiet, private sort of man, mature and clearly self-confident. His self-confidence revealed itself in the discourtesy which prompted him to continue reading his newspaper while the rest of us were participating in the business of the group. His bad manners caused some hesitation among us when we came to decide upon his acceptability, but we thought we might pass him, as in a General Election campaign his individual defects might pass un-noticed.

It was our misfortune that Mr Paterson had intended that he would stand in Berwick and East Lothian. When we came to consider candidate selection for the by-election our concern for the greater good of the Party came into conflict with Mr Paterson's expectations. Regardless of his full awareness of the rules regarding by-elections he had no notion of making way for any candidate thought more appropriate. In his stance he was supported by his local constituency officials. Clearly he, and they alike, regarded the pledge which he had accepted, as just a kind of formality, with no serious purpose.

When the Committee met we were reinforced by non-Committee members from the Parliamentary Group and national office-bearers. Mr Paterson and his C.A. Chairman sat with us, and we prepared for a very unpleasant and embarrassing experience. I knew that the MPs were against his selection and would not accept it. In the knowledge that the eventual outcome would be that Mr Paterson would be told that we were going to proceed on the specific by-election procedures, I thought it best for everyone to conclude the discussion as swiftly as possible. So, I reminded the company of the rules regarding by-elections, reminded Mr Paterson of his acceptance of the rules, and concluded with the expectation that all of us would act as loyal Party members would wish to do, and act for the greater good.

My trust in shared Party loyalty proved appallingly misplaced. Mr Paterson's refusal to step aside was fully supported by local officials. A follow-up meeting took Douglas Crawford, Stephen Maxwell, Colin Bell and myself to meet the local members, but they refused any candidate other than Mr Paterson, and instead most of them resigned from the Party.

Having denied the Party's nomination to Mr Paterson we now had to choose a candidate whose cause, never very hopeful, would now be utterly hopeless. The sort of experience we had looked for was such as offered by George Leslie and Isobel Lindsay, and these were two people with whom we now pleaded. With the most admirable and selfless courage Isobel agreed to be nominated.

This choice brought further outbursts of rage and abuse. It transpired that news had spread that Isobel was pregnant. At a National Council hate session I was denounced for nominating a woman candidate at all, and particularly one in Isobel's particular circumstances. When I said that it had never occurred to me that pregnancy was a disqualification, some of the noise subsided. It emerged that the furious faction didn't have some strange hostility to pregnancy. Their problem was that in their ignorance they did not know that Isobel was married.

The whole episode was most depressing. To have clear rules ignored, then defied, and finally abandoned as the Chairman drafted alterations, confirmed my increasing fear that we were on a downward curve.

The eventual campaign was a heroic stand as Isobel fought our battle, and Alan McKinney struggled to fill gaps left by sulking locals. It was explained to me by some of these locals that many SNP members in the constituency had once been Liberals. As Liberals they had the notion that freedom just meant doing whatever you liked, and if that didn't suit Party plans then so much the worse for the Party.

The only good memory I have is one of the most intelligent and interesting political discussions I had throughout all my years in the Party, when we sat in a hotel lounge and talked over our opinions, objections, principles and predictions. The three of us? Myself, Margo MacDonald and Roseanna Cunningham.

As the General Election drew nearer the collective behaviour of the Party's leading bodies seemed to me peculiar. The NEC and the Parliamentary Group seemed more interested in settling how each might control the other's behaviour. Group representatives emphasised that they had to act on the spot, and could not be expected to wait for NEC approval, let alone instruction. The NEC repeatedly dispatched Mrs MacDonald to confer with the Group in London. From those meetings she consistently returned complaining of the Group's hostility. The Group meanwhile complained that Margo spent most of her time in London in the company of Labour members, or ex-Labour members, especially Mr Sillars. Most NEC members were quick to offer Margo sympathy and shared indignation. It was David Rollo who asked why, since Mrs MacDonald seemed to be so badly received, some other emissary might not be appointed? As I recall, only an embarrassed silence followed.

As common sense, and common Party loyalty seemed insufficient to ensure proper co-operation between the two Party authorities, an attempt was made to produce a kind of semi-legal agreement – "Protocols" – to provide rules of conduct between them. There was even a closed-circuit TV discussion, confined to a few on either side. The rest of us were left to wonder how it had come to this.

Meanwhile the NEC persevered in considering the Party's preferred attitude to future social problems, while the strengths of the Party's position, especially the Oil campaign, had been long abandoned in favour of more selfless and virtuous causes, in whose pursuit Labour could usually outbid us, and would claim any credit going even when they failed to do so.

The Group scored occasional own goals, the most famous being Hamish Watt's deliberate and ostentatious tearing up of telegrams sent by Trade Unions seeking Party support. At the NEC there was talk of the "Gang of Four", sometimes "Gang of Five". The "Gangs" were Douglas Crawford, Douglas Henderson, Hamish Watt, usually Iain MacCormick and sometimes Winnie Ewing. Significantly the power-base of these MPs was remote from the industrial belt which the NEC was keenest to favour. On the NEC the person most sympathetic to the MPs viewpoint was Robert McIntyre, and the MP most understanding of the NEC was Gordon Wilson. Significantly these two had experience of serving on both rival bodies. Some evidence of personal animosities showed itself from time to time. For instance when Margo stood in Hamilton her team let it be known that they did not wish Winnie Ewing to appear in their campaign.

Every so often, undeserved publicity would reach the Press, apparently from leaks originating in the NEC. Demands that inquiries be made were countered by so-called "explanations". For instance, Margo claimed that there need be no deliberate leak at all, but that any one of us could have just left some minutes or other document upstairs on a bus. Willie Macrae explained that he might well sometimes leave his filing cabinets open, and some passer-by could have stumbled upon some exciting information. Either of these explanations could apply only in the event of astoundingly interested and publicity sophisticated passers-by. The truth was more obvious. As Douglas Crawford used to say when the problem re-appeared, "Cui bono?" or – "Who stands to gain?" The attempted explanations insulted the intelligence of everyone present, but in a disgraceful and cowardly conspiracy of silence no real attempt was made to unmask and restrain the culprits.

Whatever disagreements on political principles or party strategy may have sparked off these dissensions, willingness to take offence, and find issues to fight over, increased. In the North-East a highly indignant campaign was relentlessly waged against "the Central Belt" allegedly dominating the NEC. Perhaps especially in the said "Central Belt" there was instinctive hostility to any person in any office. Such a person was from time to time the victim of peddlers of suspicion and malice. It was this mood which prompted me to refuse any further nomination to any elected position within the Party, because the belief was being encouraged that anyone elected to anything was bound to be untrustworthy.

I didn't recognise it at the time, but early signs of feminist enthusiasm were apparent. Meetings increasingly seemed to be attended by numbers of young women all in a furious temper regardless of the topic under discussion. In due course there grew a campaign to change the designation of our office-bearers. Many fiery eyes and waving fists attended discussions on making the Party "Chairman" become the Party "Convener". I didn't see the point, I confess. I thought it was just another attempt to prove how trustworthily like

133

Labour we were, "Convener" being a widespread and respected title in Labour Party and municipal circles. Even once the gender significance was pointed out I still was puzzled. "Convener" is itself a masculine noun. If a female word is wanted it has to be "Conventrix". Despite my good and helpful intentions, this was regarded as being too pedantic.

Finally, when all else failed, anyone in search of a reason to dislike could fall back upon age. I learned from someone who enjoyed such knowledge, that a fellow member wanting to purge of the NEC of undesirables had held me up as a possible target. "The man has been here forever" he complained. "He must be 70 if he's a day." At the time I was 50.

Though a trivial episode, this hostility to an older generation was part of the spirit of the age. Since the '60s the idea that youth must be served had become a pretty orthodox point of view. The generation whose opinions had been formed in the war years and the immediate aftermath, was being gradually ousted by maturing men and women whose childhood and adolescence had been spent in the Cold War years, threatened by the Bomb and inclined to blame their rulers for making them so afraid. The young would do better. Women would do better. An older person in office, or in any promoted position, was an obstacle to the advance of confident and ambitious persons impatient to wait for some designated retiral age to open up prospects. Gordon has written that jealousy lay behind many of our troubles. I am utterly convinced that he is right, and I regret that we were nowhere nearly frank enough in dealing with the problem. We should have openly acknowledged it, and taken steps to remove the grievance which in any organisation grows more bitter the longer ambition is frustrated.

All of these issues came together after the General Election of 1979 left us facing the loss of 9 MPs, only Gordon Wilson and Donald Stewart surviving. Whatever the demerits of the Parliamentary Group may have been, all were at an end. The NEC would have no rival. Some of its members may well have savoured the prospect.

The 1979 debacle discredited the strategy which had been followed by the NEC since 1974 – to work towards a plan for devolution and a Scottish Assembly. It was, in the light of our Party's history, clearly a strategy of gradualism, defended and justified as such by our NEC leaders. It was Home Rule not independence. It was Home Rule Association, Scottish Party, Scottish Convention in its pedigree and its emotions. It was not Nationalist.

The immediate reaction to defeat, as happens to every defeated regime – or most at least – was to replace in office those most identified with the failed policy. No question of fairness enters into things when such times arrive. When elections to the NEC took place at the following Conference, it was clear that SNP members had turned to persons whose Nationalist credentials they had observed over the years and who for that very reason they now trusted.

Gordon Wilson, though of a younger age group, took over as Chairman, and three old guardsmen par excellence made their comeback – Robert McIntyre, Arthur Donaldson and myself. I still find it a moving fact that Party members no matter how tempted into shortcuts, do trust most those who have wavered least.

Of course, there were other opinions. One post Conference meeting was entertained by comparison with the opening of graves and calling upon ancestral spirits. Douglas Henderson himself always and totally Nationalist, nevertheless saw dangers as Gordon has recorded. The balance, Douglas reckoned, had gone too far.

CHAPTER 14

LEAVING THE THICK OF THINGS

The Labour Party had "groups", didn't they? So why shouldn't we? Even the Tories had various "clubs", with members giving their support to whichever faction best reflected their personal opinions. What was over-looked was that these were big, powerful parties, whose objective was government, power and office, competing to feather their eventual nest and make more comfortable their personal future. It was rather different for a small, aspiring Party like ours, whose aim was the attainment of a principled goal. Professional prospects did not enter into our thinking at this time. Indeed there was still a strong body of opinion in the SNP which assumed that the Party would simply disband once independence was achieved. It may seem incredible to present day members, but be assured, this was indeed the case.

So any Group, however justified by virtue of Labour's trailblazing, was going to be to some extent disturbing. When Kenneth Fee's discoveries began to be reported, misgivings increased, as statements and resolutions presenting socialist republican aspirations in a good light were increasingly revealed. Republican views, especially in the minds of those on the Left, were, and are, widespread. In those earlier days some fellow-members seemed to find in Irish republicanism a parallel to be followed. In due course the '79 Group had to be brought to order by its wiser leaders, to prevent the fostering of links with Sinn Fein. So, especially in Glasgow and the West, tempers were becoming rather sensitive.

These tendencies fed into the still evident atmosphere of hostility. Robert McIntyre, editing, for a spell, the S.I., decided against publishing an article by Billy Wolfe, his argument being that the text would require two full pages, and the theme, in his opinion, was not of sufficient interest to justify such an allocation. Nothing public was said of this event, yet, nevertheless, the S.I. was assailed in letters and statements from, more or less

136

simultaneously, Roxburgh, Inverness and Orkney. It was as if beacons blazed on hill tops to give warning of injustice. No one ever came forward to claim the credit for this further attack on the S.I.'s imperfections.

With or without Groups, we were beginning to suffer severely from our increasing failure, and, at times, refusal, to talk to one another. Many leading lights know little or nothing of the real opinions and attitudes of many of their colleagues. Quite often I found myself pleading that we must begin talking to one another again. When numbers were small we knew one another and knew our various views. Now, as we had grown, we remained in many cases strangers, uninformed about what others thought, but ignorance did not prevent quite mistaken conclusions. For instance, because of my age I was assumed by many to be some sort of old Tory, an opinion held by those whom I had never met or spoken to. What I thought about things, they had no real idea, so sometimes they just made it up.

Several of us were now emerging as targets for the dislike of the growing and powerful force combining principally under the influence of Mrs MacDonald. Those who had incurred her criticism or dislike were now especially at risk of attack. Her chilly relationship with Winnie was no secret. She clashed regularly with Douglas Crawford, and Robert McIntyre she memorably described, in a Conference aside, as "that bloody old spider". One interesting aspect of Margo's position at this time, was that she was head and shoulders above her associates. She had no peers, just supporters. Jim Sillars was not yet a member and Alex Salmond had not fully emerged into leadership status.

By the time the festering ill-feeling came to a head, it was not wholly clear who the potential controllers of the Party wanted rid of. Newcomers to the NEC naturally fell into the trap always awaiting fair-minded people. "I will judge everyone as I find them" goes the argument, and thus the experiences of others are of no effect. As one particularly nasty meeting was nearing its end, Neil MacCormick tried to find the words to bring a harmonious end to the acrimony, and, my own temper having frayed, I warned that they wanted rid of him as well as me, and could hardly wait. Interestingly enough, I had a letter from Billy Wolfe after that meeting, expressing his sympathy for what he saw as the "hurt" which I felt. He explained that when people showed contempt for him he would respond in kind. Whether he thought I was being punished, and if so for what, wasn't clear, but at least he did feel some sort of placatory words were called for.

However by now I was as combative as those who sat glaring at me across the room. Kenneth Fee's researches had brought him to conclude that there might be a frank and open expression of opposition to the '79 Group, its methods and its programme. One open meeting was held in the Stakis Hotel in Stirling after a National Council meeting. I went along to learn what the arguments were, but, being hostile to divisive organisations, I felt no urge to involve myself. As the months passed however, one vital fact preyed on my mind more and more. I realised that I had not heard Nationalist attitudes from an SNP platform for years. Our arguments and energies seemed devoted to serving causes shared by others, while principles and suggestions particularly and specifically ours were never aired.

When another meeting was convened by Kenneth, again in Stirling, I attended, and committed myself to supporting what came to be called the "Campaign for Nationalism in Scotland". As delegates and observers enjoyed the relaxed aftermath of the National Council meeting, I was among those who heard from some young colleagues the comment that Wallace was a knight and therefore a class enemy, and that they themselves were "Socialists, not Nationalists". We seemed some steps along the way towards a Party in the image of Brian Wilson, Jack McConnell or worse.

Kenneth devised the necessary publicity for the new organisation, and prepared for its launch as a fringe event at the forthcoming Annual conference in Ayr.

Gordon recalls his opinions about these tensions within the Party by this stage. He states that he "knew from sources that the '79 Group was in steep decline with splits arising on the republican issue." If this was the case it was far from evident to me, and it is unfortunate that more of us were left without such information and reassurance. The

138

posture and public statements from relevant persons seemed every bit as truculent as at any time. Their unconcealed ill-will and their ill-considered conclusions, especially on defence and diplomacy, had led me already to give up trying to return Dundee East to election-fighting potential, because our organisation was no longer in a fit state to fight. For this to happen in the constituency of our Party Chairman, which he and we actually held, was an open proof of the destruction which alternative enthusiasms and factions had brought upon us.

The meeting which Kenneth had organised was duly held. He explained his purpose and the steps by which he had come to his conclusions. There followed speeches from Winnie Ewing, Robert McIntyre, Gordon Murray and myself. As I sat listening to my colleagues I became aware that we all had our own particular reasons for our presence, and my own anger at the neglect of Nationalist-based statements and policies was not necessarily matched in the emotions of the others.

It still seemed to me a justified and interesting meeting, allowing at least for an open exchange of views instead of sneaky and often quite erroneous allegations. As the meeting proceeded, the room had filled up and by question time the presence of many '79 Group members, supporters, friends and relatives was apparent. The questions left me totally ignored. All the contributions focussed upon the merits of Groups, and why some speakers saw the '79 Group as somehow needing to be protected. One lady kept on at Winnie. "Please Winnie" she repeated, maintaining a semblance of courtesy, because no one would publicly seek to bring ridicule or hostility upon the most famous of all Nationalists.

I had no expectation that the Groups – '79 or any other – should be banned. Things had gone far beyond that stage. What I now wanted was a frank opening of debate, undeterred by fears of "washing dirty linen", to allow us, as I had long urged, to talk to one another. We couldn't now do it in calm and comradely fashion, but let us do it, if we must, as angry but convinced and honest adversaries.

Still arguing about Groups, the company dispersed. Two journalists acknowledged me as I left. One was an old University friend, Charlie Graham, of the "Express". He and I had collaborated in schools' debating competitions. It was at one of his "Express" debates that I met my two fellow judges, Neville Garden, journalist and critic, and Dermot McQuarrie from, I think, the BBC. It was at that meeting that Mr McQuarrie remarked that if the SNP ever came to hold office, "the streets of Scotland would run with Catholic blood." He didn't explain.

However, past friendships, in these times of new and up-to-date divisions, counted for nothing. Charlie frowning upon me, said "You will regret this day's work."

The other press man finishing off his notes, was Chris Baur. I didn't know him personally but everyone who ever read a paper knew him by sight and repute. As one might do at the end of a frank and lively meeting, I smiled and nodded to him. He glared upon me with anger and hate written all over his features.

Perhaps Charlie had a point. Winnie Ewing was never really vilified because that just couldn't be done. Kenneth Fee was gradually socially rehabilitated because of his wit and brilliance in Party gatherings. Gordon Murray didn't care tuppence what his critics felt, and he went his own way as was his usual custom. Robert McIntyre was eventually absolved from hate by virtue of growing to an advanced age.

All my colleagues thus found forgiveness. As for me there are several prominent SNP personalities who have not spoken to me since that day.

For a short time it seemed that our challenge had met with partial success. The Chairman tabled an emergency resolution with the intention of banning all Groups within the Party. The resolution was carried, but its effect was diluted within a very few months. The steps towards conclusion of the dispute are traced by Gordon. Individuals who defied the instruction to disband their group were then faced, first with expulsion, then with suspension. The Campaign for Nationalism obeyed the resolution immediately. Siol nan

140

Gaidheal ignored it, and were in due course declared an organisation whose members were ineligible for Party membership. The '79 Group adopted a series of devices to evade the consequences of the ruling. As time passed opinion within the Party was sensed by the Chairman as willing a conclusion to the whole business. A conciliatory motion saved face and allowed the '79 Group leaders to return to full acceptable restored membership. Only Margo MacDonald refused to accept. Her fame and popularity with the public allowed her to be indifferent to the wishes and instructions of the Party. She returned briefly to the Party's ranks when the Scottish Parliament was established and the Party's nomination was helpful. Fairly soon her determination to be guided by her own reasoning once again made her an awkward colleague, and she and her colleagues went their own ways. She has always been well aware of her power which makes any attempt at Party-imposed discipline quite futile. Her election as an avowed Independent merely rounded off her assertion of freedom from Party control.

Gordon puts the best possible gloss on the outcome of the civil war. He seems to accept the idea that compromise was achieved, that "the four years of internecine warfare" had ended and that in unity the Party could recover.

As for my own position I played no part other than paying membership dues and helping at election times or at Party events as called upon. Once when I looked ahead to retirement from work, I anticipated working unpaid and as nearly full-time as requested, for the Party. As it turned out, by the time I retired the Party's managers didn't even want me as a member.

CHAPTER 15

SOME REGRETS

Labour governments have become laughable in recent years because when they suffer defeat, frustration, humiliation or embarrassment, their answer has been "let's move on" or "let's draw a line under that." It settles nothing, and is really brazen in its effrontery, and yet sometimes that weaselly and deceitful advice is sound. Sometimes decisions are taken with which we do not agree, but in reality there is no going back to re-think attitudes or reverse decisions.

I have disagreed with the Party's decisions on some basic issues. For instance, I thought that Mr George Robertson was right when he predicted that devolution would kill "stone dead" Nationalist hopes for independence. I certainly took it for granted that such was Labour's motive for allowing things to go so far. There were those in the Labour Party who proffered support for devolution, and SNP opinion at the highest level had favoured the argument that independence was most likely to arrive after the Party had proved itself capable of government. I resented having to pass tests and earn the condescension of Britain's rulers before being "given" independence as some sort of reward for good behaviour. My resentment mattered not one whit, and was shared, as it seemed, by no one in high office in the Party. I am sorry that events have taken the course they have, but I feel no duty to try to go back to the position as it was. We have, indeed, "moved on", and must make the best of things, even though Robertson may well turn out to be right.

I also believed, and still do, that the Party, especially its Parliamentarians, made an unwise choice when they sponsored the vote of no confidence which brought down the Labour government in 1979. There was no need for their action. There were many escape routes open to them. We might have lost face by thundering threats and then doing nothing, but our red faces would have lasted for a very short time and been soon forgotten. For us to be left looking a bit foolish, would have given Labour great pleasure, but it would have been infinitely less damaging to us than our role which remains to this day their noisiest propaganda weapon against us. Again it is past, and we can do nothing to alter the course which events have taken.

Some other follies we have committed. We have drifted into accepting the concept of "referendum" which really does not fit with a parliamentary system. It was a device introduced by the master of evasion, Harold Wilson, who saw that his party would disrupt itself if it had to decide for or against membership of the EEC. A referendum removed any obligation to make public choice. Clever, but really a one-off dodge, which should never have been allowed to be thought of as a future part of our political process. We in particular were doubly foolish. Firstly we campaigned for what was glaringly going to be the losing side, and with some very unattractive allies, then we have gone on to speak humbly and submissively of the use of the referendum device for ever more, even though, with all the powers of the state, the media and money against us, we will always lose many more than we win. Again, what's done is done, and we can only grin and bear it. But what simpletons we can be.

So, sometimes we have been trapped by the political system within which we have to operate. Sometimes we have been outwitted by those who make its rules. But sometimes we have made rods for our own backs.

Scotland is a small country with a small population. Depart from pretty well any point on its mainland at dawn, and you can be pretty sure of being home by bedtime. Why then are we so tempted to make a great fuss about imagined diversity? We are Scotland's National Party. Why, then, do we so often sound as though our part of Scotland must command some loyalty denied to other parts? Remember how the enemies of independence divide us when decisions are called for. Orkney and Shetland are urged into secession, especially if the oil is Shetland's, not Scotland's. The parochial banter which is innocent and comical, can too easily become damaging. I have sat through NEC meetings, and have been dispatched on NEC missions, dealing with preposterous notions of conflicting advantage between especially the North East and "the Central Belt" – a phrase which from too many in the North East corner sounds like a term of abuse.

143

This localism is pointless and damaging. Any clash of interests stands to be resolved by reflection over policy decisions and we should never give a hearing to those who seek to turn them into a clash of emotions over rival or hostile patriotisms.

Then, as if our fundamental cause was not noble enough, we have, some of us, managed to find causes nobler still. In the past, Christian divisions were given an importance above politics. In the present too, for many, this ranking of principles still applies. Where religion once prevailed over mere politics, we now find some cause enjoying the kind of awe and reverence once granted only to religion.

In the United States, during the years before the Civil War, American statesman, William Seward, brought upon himself much abuse. When slave owners argued that the Constitution gave them the right to hold slaves, Seward replied that there was "a higher law" than the Constitution. The shock and horror, much sincere, much feigned, which his remark caused, possibly cost him the Presidency.

Some of us have gone looking for some higher law, or a cause on some higher moral plane. For some, Socialism was the cause of choice. For some it was pacifism, and in particular, Nuclear Disarmament. There can be little likelihood of disagreement when we claim that no independent Scotland would ever seek any nuclear weapon. This, at the simplest, is a mere matter of money and public health. But when it is turned into some sort of moral obligation the arguments tend to drift back in time, and demand consideration of the rights and wrongs of decisions taken in 1945. It is divisive to demonise a generation which was grateful to have its young men saved from deaths on Japanese beaches. Move on. Stop finding some moral fault in those of us close enough to these events to feel no obligation to join you in anachronistic penitence.

The high level of anger and enmity, which attends argument on the nuclear weapons issue, has had an effect upon our opinions of the wider world. For reasons of language, history, family ties, cultural familiarity, financial advantage, and no doubt others, it ought

144

to be our wish and purpose to be on good terms with the United States. But repeatedly we have placed ourselves alongside their critics and even their enemies.

It is understandable that America is unpopular with so many. Its voters in 1980, 1984 and 1988 gave Presidential, and, usually, congressional power to the most ruthless and chauvinistic elements in America. The dominant politicians then placed in the Supreme Court, judges whose opinions were on the wilder extremes of Conservative opinion. In 1992 and 1996 a popular President frittered away his opportunities and in 2000 the Supreme Court gave the Presidency to a man who was not elected. His policies have condemned his country and its allies to disasters of war and depression. It is not possible to feel happiness or affection when we look at the USA as moulded by George W. Bush, his courtiers, and the grotesque irresponsibles of Fox News.

Here it's not a matter of "let's move on", but rather of looking back, to better times and better people. Once Franklin Roosevelt presided, and could be called the leader of the Free World without anyone sniggering. Once there was Harry Truman, ridiculed and hated by the most high and mighty and rich in the land, but who defiantly and gallantly was able to retire with honour, and to be treated by history as one who had confronted and eventually overcome his critics. There was John F. Kennedy, so welcomed by the world, honoured by people who from the jungle brought ceremonial robes to be offered for his funeral. There was Lyndon Johnson, who remembered as a young teacher the hardships and deprivations of his pupils, and who remembered how racial supremacy had been exercised. As President, he led the political battle against these evils, and left a victory which the modern Supreme Court and its allies are still struggling to reverse.

We don't have any power to affect American events or to help the current President against the forces of prejudice and absurdity which menace him. Our opinions are all we have to offer. Let us not waste them in grumbling about some less attractive features of American society and past conduct. It is in Scotland's interests to secure and maintain the best possible relations with the strongest power in the kind of world to which our country belongs.

Obviously my regrets over some policies and some decisions spring from my feeling that we too often have failed to appreciate the realities of Scotland's situation in relation to other countries or to events and processes going on around us. For a short time I was identified as Convener of the Party's External Affairs Committee. It proved a futile body, because Party policy-makers didn't judge our interests accurately, but preferred to indulge in the diplomatic equivalent of street demonstrations. We were thought obliged to assume that we were inevitably bound to favour all movements which seemed similar to ours. So, when Winnie Ewing made allies of the parties who governed France and Ireland, the NEC, most office-bearers, and many members, were quick to deplore her choice. Under the barrage of criticism she was pressured into making allies of some smaller groups in the European Parliament. Some of them were decent enough, but none of them gave Scotland the kind of entry into the councils of those rulers who could do us many useful favours. We preferred to preserve our purity, unsullied by the coarse efficiency of Gaullist and Fianna Fail ministers.

Despite Winnie's influence in the Party, and even when that powerful influence combined with that of Gordon Wilson, a sensible, realistic policy on our relations with Europe was achieved only when Jim Sillars brought his thinking and voice to bear upon the problem, and swept the Party into the "Independence in Europe" position. Much of Jim Sillars's influence was beneficial. Putting a stop to the prolonged anti-European rhetoric was helpful. He was also worth his place in Party history when he gave the power of his backing to help to keep the Party out of the trap which Donald Dewar had prepared for us. So the Party derived benefit from his membership, even apart from his by-election victory.

He did have one blind spot. He briefly seemed to be carried away, as many over-excitable and unrealistic Nationalists before him had been, and talked and acted as if we were on some sort of exciting verge of revolution. He called for a campaign of "civil disobedience", and talked up the notion of "the Scottish Resistance". He had got kind of carried away. Scots to an overwhelming extent were wholly unimpressed by such imagery. They did not feel oppressed. Perhaps they should, but they didn't, and don't. And it was absurdly easy for our opponents to express horror at any threats of lawlessness. Only in relation to non-payment of the Poll Tax did any resistance materialise.

As for Defence, CND loyalties and anti-American prejudice have made rational consideration of Scotland's relations with NATO impossible. Consideration of our best interests remains prohibited. At one time the NEC had given support to the notion that an independent Scotland must not join a military alliance to deter aggressors. Rather let the aggressor come, and then take to the hills and fight a guerrilla war for years if need be. It didn't seem to occur to those who put forward the suggestion, that the deaths and suffering such a war would cause would have been the most dreadful of military outcomes. None the less, speeches from leading figures urged such nonsense upon us, and nodding heads and serious, deep-thinking expressions indicated how seriously they took their ideas. Fortunately the debate on Defence has moved on to more rational topics like the nuclear submarine base at Faslane. The Party was curiously slow to turn its attention to Faslane because it was so noisily and fervently denouncing the Americans in the Holy Loch. In the S.I. it was pointed out that the Americans would leave when the need for the Holy Loch was gone, but the British would stay in Faslane for ever, because they thought it was theirs. As an obstacle to our independence the British state far surpasses America.

CHAPTER 16

THE SCOTS INDEPENDENT AND THE PARTY

I used to ask NEC colleagues how much our fellow Party members knew of the plans and decisions which we made and took on their behalf. I suspected that the answer was "very little". After 1983 I learned that my suspicions were correct. Since that time I have known no more about the Party than is on public record, available to anyone who is at all interested. So I have very little to say to posterity about the Party's hard times in the 1980s, or about the political developments which brought the issue of Scottish government once more to the top of the Parliamentary agenda.

Probably the most significant pointer to the future came with Jim Sillars's victory in the Govan by-election in 1988. I was in America during the entire duration of that campaign, but before I left I predicted, to various witnesses, that he would win. As I attended election meetings and rallies in various cities and states, and sat through TV reports and debates, I felt sure that I had prophesised correctly. Mr Sillars's political talents and skills seemed vastly superior to those displayed by Vice-President George H.W. Bush and Governor Michael Dukakis. The American people seemed to feel as I did that they had little to enthuse over in either candidate. I returned to Prestwick just as Sillars's victory was reported. Having watched a nasty and worthless campaign, culminating in the election of the candidate most responsible for these characteristics, I felt that if Jim Sillars had been operating on the American stage he would have been elected President. In comparison, he would have deserved to be.

I made these opinions known in a report which I wrote for the Scots Independent, and my political activities now became centred on that paper.

I had been connected with the S.I. since 1955 when it passed into the care of the private company chaired by Dr McIntyre, replacing the previous joint control arrangement. For the next 50 years the paper has been maintained thanks to the loyal and committed support and labour, of people whose names merit inclusion in any SNP roll of honour.

The paper has never received money from the Party, nor have any of its directors ever received any money for their work. Unable to maintain paid staff on any scale, or for any length of time, volunteers handled most of the necessary work. Robert McIntyre himself led the way for many years, and the paper's premises and trading arrangements fell to such stalwarts as Murdoch Young and Robert Campbell. For 50 years the business of the company was looked after by Tom Preston from Airdrie, who made his vital work for the S.I. his own personal contribution to the Party's cause.

From an early stage Tom found a kindred spirit to keep the Stirling end of any business arrangements under trusted supervision when Archie Young joined the team. Every aspect of the paper's work gained from the arrival in the area of Gordon Boyd, an absolute dynamo of happy, energetic effort. Gordon had been active in his native North-East, in the Covenant Association. On the Party's behalf he now arranged for Arthur Donaldson to undertake the work as candidate in Kinross and West Perthshire, effectively making a start to the process which has enabled us to hold Perthshire seats in two Parliaments. When he left Blackford and returned to the North-East, he galvanised things to such an extent that Alex Farquhar came within a remarkably small percentage of winning East Aberdeenshire. Gordon was one who lingers forever in the memory.

A new generation enabled the paper to function unbroken despite many crises. Peter Wright chaired the Board for several years, and took responsibility for seeing to the dispatch of each month's edition to branches, C.A.s and agents throughout the country. Bobby Littlejohn of Stirling, Russell Irwin of Dumbarton and now, Denholm Christie of Kincardine, served as Company secretaries. As colleague and successor to Tom Preston there came Ian Hamilton, famous as Chief Steward of Conferences and as an active contributor to the Party in Moray constituency.

Several professional journalists edited the paper, Michael Grieve, Dougie Stewart, Donnie MacMillan, Alwyn James and Colin Bell, all giving long service. But from within the S.I.'s own ranks, editors were found as need arose. Most remarkably, Kenneth

Fee took on the task in what was seen as an emergency, and stayed in post, cherishing a few enemies, but making hundreds of friends, for his paper, for just on 20 years.

An exciting and stimulating interlude was the year in which Professor James Taggart and Dr Jenny Herriot were jointly responsible. They gave the Board new aspirations and encouraged new ambitions. We lacked the means to follow through on their plans, and we had to call upon another "temporary" editor, Jim Lynch, who is still there, as enthusiastic as if on his first day at his desk.

There are, of course, snags in running a paper controlled by people who are Party members, but who are not under instructions from the NEC or Party office-bearers. There have been occasions when the paper has given an airing to some report or suggestion which has displeased the Party's leaders.

Robert and Kenneth and I were all unpopular with the leaders who emerged as the winners from the internal rows of the '80s. In particular they were on the keenest possible look-out for any contradictions to their wishes which Kenneth Fee might allow to appear in print. This distrust prompted the NEC to tell the S.I. Board that they should give the NEC the power to appoint the editor of the S.I. Such an arrangement would have left the Board with no real purpose, and was, in business terms, an impossible alternative to present to a private company.

We had some exchanges over these matters, and two formally convened meetings. At the first, the Board met with Alex Salmond, Jim Sillars and Tom McAlpine. We had refused to surrender the power to appoint the editor, so the NEC now sought to find some other way to protect themselves from any material appearing in the S.I. which might seem, as they put it, "counter productive". Legally, we had no shares to sell to anyone seeking to become a director, nor could we guarantee that shareholders would agree to the election of any such person even if a way was found to nominate him or her.

We did see a reasonable way to reassure the NEC by offering to allow an observer from their ranks, to attend S.I. Board meetings. This seemed feasible, but of course we had our own reassurance to consider, and did not see much wisdom in inviting someone whose hostility to the paper was unconcealed. So, by advising Mr Salmond that he would not be acceptable, we did not exactly conciliate. Fortunately our ill-wishers were not able to be totally frank, and we were able to suggest an acceptable person, who would not have been their preferred choice but whom they would have been embarrassed to refuse. So it came about, that Dr Allan McArtney who had himself edited the paper on several occasions, was invited to join Kenneth Fee when the material was being prepared for publication. Kenneth referred to Allan thereafter as "our censor", and editorial meetings, I understand, became very happy and sociable.

A further meeting was ordered by the NEC when some unacceptable item was printed, and we were summoned to answer for our offence. Denholm Christie and I met with three NEC representatives, two of whom had been politically and personally friendly to us, and who thus showed some embarrassment at having to chastise us. John Swinney and Allan McArtney seemed ready to accept our regret that we had offended Michael Russell, however, was angry enough to warn that good relations would be impaired if the NEC found the S.I. constantly "nipping at our ankles". As, by that time, we had ample reason to conclude that the NEC of the time had passed to C.A.s and branches their wish that they would no longer buy the paper, I felt entitled and free to reply in kind. If we were seen to be nipping at ankles, we believed that the NEC's biting at our throat was a much greater injury.

It was all very inconclusive. But the answer to these hostilities, just as in the days of NEC v Parliamentary Group battles, did not come from agreements negotiated and documented. The answer came as time passed, controversies changed, and personal influences became important. During the Taggart period the S.I. had published some very substantial articles, critical of the Party's policies and leaders and suggesting alternative strategies. This provision of a platform for those dissenting from the Party's leadership did not make for harmony. It was even reported that at the highest Party levels Kenneth Fee was remembered as a much-missed friend.

The various Party chiefs, who had expressed displeasure with the paper, had never understood that the S.I. had never been critical of any tactic or policy which was in keeping with the commitment to secure independence. On other, off-target issues and opinions, we might feel free to disagree. We also could claim, as I indeed did at our second meeting, that our collective record of service and loyalty made us as much an authentic voice of the movement as an NEC, here today, and with every possibility of being gone tomorrow – or at least after the next Conference.

Some reassurance that the S.I. was not wilfully insubordinate gradually dawned upon the Party's officials. When Jim Lynch became editor, the political timetable for years to come was already known, and elections would be recurring at regular intervals. With our total agreement, he made it clear that the S.I. would never allow itself to be used as a base from which critics would mount an attack on the Party, or those responsible for its management.

Whatever help we could give, and whatever loyalty we could express, were pledged to the Party. This pledge would be called into question in one event only, - if the Party ever discarded independence as its goal and its purpose.

About 30 years ago I had a conversation with Billy Wolfe, prompted by looking at one of our old traditional membership cards. The first pledge was to work for Scottish independence. I wondered if anything else was really necessary, and if the little addendum about "defending Scotland's interests" in general could not, quite justly, be taken for granted. Should we not consider doing away with it therefore? Billy, who always liked the wider view, did not favour the idea, and asked why I did. My answer was that I feared that, some day, support for that second clause might be used to justify or excuse dilution of support for the first. It has not yet happened but the threat has been suggested by the press within the very recent past. Promptly corrected by the First

Minister, misquoted and misinterpreted, the report should still be noted as a very damaging dispute in the making.

The important fact is that the S.I. is a willing asset for the Party in the political battles to come, and will always be while we pursue the same goal.

CHAPTER 17

FROM NOW ON

One text which Nationalist speakers must all have used in their time, came from the masthead of Oliver Brown's paper, "Scots Socialist". It read, "We are not British. We are Scots. We are Europeans. We are citizens of the World." There is not, for a democratic Scottish Nationalist, much more to be said. Our goal, our principles and our view of our cause are all covered.

These words were repeated recently from a "Scots Independent" platform, in the presence of Oliver's daughters and grand-daughter. Every year the S.I. makes the Oliver Brown Award to some person who has in some way encouraged Scots to find pride and confidence in the service of their country. The list of recipients is now impressive and significant.

The idea of the Award came from our then Editor, Colin Bell. Editors tend to leave some permanent reminder of their days in office. The Award was Colin's.

In his turn, Kenneth Fee envisaged and organised readers and subscribers to the paper, into forming a Fellowship, to keep the S.I. existing and working towards our objective. The Fellows have enabled the paper to survive, and no support can surpass that.

Jim Lynch, during his tenure, has built up the S.I.'s website. We have called it "The Flag in the Wind". John MacCormick used the vision of the unconquered Flag still bravely flying, even though years of disappointment continue to pass. But the flag is still there. There are thousands of Saltires to be seen now in communities where once they were rarities.

Yet, today a History course being conducted by Dundee University, undertakes to explain to students, the making of "The British Nation". We know there is a British state, but we know there is no British nation. There is no Scandinavian nation. There is no Iberian

154

nation, nor states either. But there are Norway and Sweden, and Denmark too. There are Spain and Portugal. There are nations with flags and history and memory and identity. We qualify to join them and it is our task to persevere until we do. "Britain" is a fact of Geography but a temporary invention of History.